Challenging
the Church
MONSTER

Challenging
the Church
MONSTER

From Conflict to Community

Douglas J. Bixby

The Pilgrim Press

Cleveland

To my wife Carolyn Bixby
Your love, support, beauty, intellect, patience, and commitment
help me to be who I am and do what I do.

The Pilgrim Press, 700 Prospect Avenue East, Cleveland, Ohio 44115-1100

pilgrimpress.com

© 2002 by Douglas J. Bixby

Printed in the United States of America on acid-free paper

06   05   04   03   02   5   4   3   2   1

Library of Congress Cataloging-in-Publication Data

Bixby, Douglas J., 1967-
   Challenging the church monster : from conflict to community / Douglas J. Bixby.
      p.   cm.
   Includes bibliographical references.
   ISBN 0-8298-1506-6 (pbk. : alk. paper)
   1. Church controversies.   2. Church management.   3. Conflict management—Religious aspects—Christianity.   I. Title.

BV652.9 .B59   2002
250—dc21
                                                                              2002034582

Contents

Foreword

This book is especially for you if you ever have left a church meeting wondering if anything was accomplished; had two weeks to go before the Sunday-school year began and needed six more teachers; wondered why a certain, apathetic church member agreed to serve on the church council; assumed that it is the pastor's job to make sure that everything in the church gets done; awakened in the middle of the night worrying about your committee being prepared for its next big project; spent two months getting a new-church initiative ready, only to have it voted down; thought that your church was putting the cart before the horse; or tried to inspire others at church but ended up just as discouraged as they were.

This book is especially for you if any of the above scenarios describe something that has happened to you. In the language of this book, you would have experienced being attacked by the "church monster." To author and pastor Douglas Bixby, there are too many church monsters lurking around today's congregations. These monsters, he argues, are the "overgrown, complicated church structures" that get in the way of authentic ministry. Bixby wants to help your church to tame this monster and get on with its intended purpose: to proclaim and enact the love and justice that God has revealed in Jesus Christ.

Why is the topic—rather, the metaphor—of church monsters a fitting one these days? Simply put, it is because so many congregations in North America are losing their energy and ministry effectiveness. Those of us who are old enough to remember the 1960s realize that our society has been doing a lot of changing in the last few generations. I don't know about you, but some of those changes I like, and some of them I do not like. Our churches are the same way: They find it easier to accept certain social changes but not others. Congregations—and those members—who have been around a long time find it hard to adjust. The conditions in their community that once supported their beloved church in its heyday do not last forever. Nothing ever does—except the love of God. Often it is hard for churches to realize that they do not have to like the changes that they see around them. But if their gospel witness is to continue over time, churches need to do something about the changes that do occur.

A recent television commercial for the latest electronic wizardry ends with the tagline, "Technology for the agile business." The word "agile" is not one that we use much, but we know what it means. To be agile is to be nimble, fleet of foot, able to move quickly and easily, as circumstances demand. Douglas Bixby is one pastor who believes that churches need to be agile, too. He claims that doing something about cumbersome church organizational structure is one key to keeping our collective Christian witness agile.

The church monster of complicated church structures distracts us from the main purpose for their creation: to help our churches actually do ministry. Bixby mentions that, in days gone by, people had more time to get involved with "large bureaucratic church governments." But time, while an obvious practical factor, is not the only reason that church structures can become distracting. I was talking once with a successful dentist who was a lifelong member of his church. "They asked me to serve on the church board once, and I served only one term," he confessed to me. "I just don't like all the church politics." In part, this faithful, discerning Christian was reflecting a frustration with the machinery itself.

Douglas Bixby wants your church to "downsize and centralize" its structures and processes for a good reason. He is not motivated merely by a concern for efficiency, to eliminate unnecessary meetings and structures. His goal is to see more churches doing what they are called to do. Early in this book, he asserts, "The structure of our churches should help us effectively manage ministry in the midst of our diversity." The story that he tells about a church stove helps to make the point: The way that we Christians do things does make a big difference—to commitment, to long-term participation, to outcome, and to satisfaction. One of the church monster's products is burnout, which does not help any church keep up its energy for ministry.

In supporting his claims, Pastor Bixby draws on the experiences of other pastors who have been surveying the American-church scene and have seen the handwriting on the wall. Although he will encourage you to take a leap of faith and make a dramatic structural change in your church, Bixby knows that it will take time for your church to adjust. It takes time to give a new, streamlined process a chance, to discover that you truly can trust others to follow through. Bixby's account of bamboo scaffolding that withstood a storm when the steel scaffolding was shattered, illustrates the importance of being flexible—even with a new structure.

In focusing on the church's structure, Bixby echoes the wisdom of some organizational theorists of our day. Keeping an organization's structure from getting too complex and rigid is one strategy for keeping that organization's energy stimulated. If members are too busy "running the maze," they don't have time to pay attention to what is most vital: that organization's basic purpose and goals.[1] In other words, the structures should serve the organization, not the other way around. Otherwise, you are creating a monster, one that devours good intentions, good people, and good opportunities for Christian ministry.

Actually, some of the earliest insights about the problems that Bixby addresses in this book go back a century or so. The great sociologist Max Weber looked across history and noted a distinction in human communities between what he called "movements" and "institutions." Movements—whether they are political, social, or even religious—often begin around one person. This dynamic leader articulates a vision and draws people to the cause. The organization at that point is quite loose and depends heavily on the dynamic leader. As time goes by, however, the leader eventually dies. If the movement is to survive, it has to take on a flavor and quality that modifies—and even moderates—the character of the movement's early fire. That is, the movement becomes an "institution"; it settles into a structured way of life that enhances its survival.[2]

Weber's early observations about common tendencies in how we humans organize ourselves help us to appreciate what Bixby promotes here. Most of our churches these days do not have trouble with being too much like movements. Rather, they tend to have become institutionalized, so much so that sometimes the spirited vigor of a particular congregation's early years has vanished. In Weber's terms, our churches need to find ways to balance the benefits of the movement with the benefits of the institution. In order to do this, Bixby calls our churches to divest themselves of the most monstrous artifacts of our institutionalization: our convoluted church structures.

Challenging the Church Monster joins a fast-growing list of diverse church resources that has emerged in the last ten to fifteen years. These resources concentrate on the congregation as a real-life (not just "spiritual") phenomenon that needs to be understood on its own terms. It might be interesting to some readers to discover that scholarly research on local churches has mushroomed since the 1980s.[3] Just as significant, however, are the books, videotapes, and training programs that are now available for practical use by churches (a small number of them are listed in Bixby's bibliography at the end of this book).

A careful reader of any of this literature will notice that the discussion does not sound purely "religious." That is, helpful insights for strong churches are also grounded in sociological research, organizational theory, group-process skills, and other so-called "secular" sources. I think that this is a good thing. Too often, church people—pastors and members alike—act as though being religious or spiritual has nothing to do with any other aspect of being human. I disagree, as do many of my scholarly colleagues. If we believe that "the Word became flesh and lived among us" (Jn 1:14a), then surely we can benefit from any kind of knowledge about our humanity and our life together, regardless of its source. Actually, I think that careful observers who do not have a religious axe to grind sometimes make more astute judgments about religious behavior than we religious people do. Sometimes, we need a big dose of seeing the way things are (*descriptive* view) before we can be smart about pursuing in our churches the way that things should be (*normative* view).

Whether you listen to both kinds of voices or not, I hope that you realize that taking good care of congregations is becoming serious business! It is becoming increasingly clear that pastors and their churches need assistance to keep churches alive and well. At the same time, don't expect that helping your church will be easy. If you follow Bixby's advice, you will meet resistance. Churches get used to things being a certain way, even if they are structures and processes that are cumbersome.

Beyond the matter of resistance to change, there is one other significant source of resistance, depending on your congregation's larger tradition. Church denominations represent three basic forms of governance (also known as "polity"), and these will influence the ways in which your specific congregation can follow Bixby's plan. The one form that will be easiest to adapt is often called *congregational.* This term refers to the authority being centered in the congregation itself, with no structure beyond the local setting having any binding force. All kinds of Baptists, as well as Congregationalist, Disciples of Christ, Church of Christ, United Church of Christ, the Evangelical Covenant, and other similar traditions live by congregational polity. This allows the greatest flexibility in all matters, including how to structure the local church.

The other two basic polities would have to modify Bixby's plan somewhat in order to benefit from it. These two are the representative form and the Episcopal form. The *episcopal* form (notice the small "e") is easily recognized through its office of bishop; the most well known examples are Roman Catholic and Anglican or Episcopalian. Bishops exercise wide authority in these and other such denominations, from pastoral appointments to many administrative duties. Depending on the denomination's other required structures, a parish or church in episcopal polity might be limited to changes that it could make to its boards and committees. In a similar way, *representative* polity clearly affects the shape of local churches' structures and processes. Reformed, Presbyterian, and like denominations tend to cover all the bases concerning operating structures. Here, Bixby's plan probably cannot be followed to the letter, but his overall purpose certainly can help to adjust and streamline the local church's processes.

If you want to appreciate the full impact of Bixby's ideas, you might want to consider reading this book's two parts in reverse order. In Part 2, he makes it clear that structural change is not an end in itself. Eventually, it must be undergirded by indications that the church is excited about its vision. A simpler church structure can encourage your church to direct its energy toward being clear about its call into God's future. Vision is the central—but not the only—factor for every dynamic congregation. Vision helps keep the congregation flexible and responsive to needs and new opportunities.[4]

Douglas Bixby writes as a ministry practitioner, one who has spent years in the day-to-day activities and pursuits of parish life. He argues for his proposal using straightforward biblical theology, heavily informed by the Pauline epistles. He directs his ideas not to scholars of the church, but to that much broader communion of saints. I often call them "the real people of the church"—and, if you are a member of a church, I mean you. You and your pastors are Rev. Bixby's best audience. If *Challenging the Church Monster* is helpful to you in the way that its author intends, it will usher your congregation into a fresh—and perhaps unexpected—experience of God's profound grace.

George B. Thompson Jr.
Associate Professor, Church Administration and Leadership
The Interdenominational Theological Center
Atlanta, Georgia

Preface

The ideas and concepts presented in this book have grown primarily out of my experience as the pastor of Salem Covenant Church in Washington, Connecticut. I started my ministry at this church immediately following seminary. Prior to entering pastoral ministry, I had virtually no experience working with church governments. However, I did have what I like to refer to as "common-sense ideas" about how things ought to function organizationally within a church. These principles were applied at Salem Covenant Church, and I later discovered that others perceived these common-sense ideas as innovative, refreshing, and helpful.

Through the image of the church monster, I seek to personify a wide variety of problems that have arisen in local churches as a result of overgrown church systems and heightened levels of conflict. Conflict will always be a part of our churches on some level. However, we should not be overwhelmed by the amount of anxiety in our church systems. It is my hope that this book will help churches deal with conflict and defeat the church monster.

At Salem Covenant Church, we have addressed several core issues by downsizing and centralizing our church government and by developing a radical commitment to congregational decision making. This book invites you to open your church up to the real and exciting possibilities that emerge from these two principles. Two of the most exciting possibilities that arise for pastors and laypeople alike are fewer meetings and more ministry, less conflict and more community.

The first half of this book describes the problems this type of restructuring seeks to address, the two key elements of this restructuring, and several ways to effectively introduce these changes. The second half focuses on moving forward. Where does a church go once restructuring has taken place? It offers practical advice on how to take advantage of the opportunities that emerge from these structural changes, some advice about leadership challenges facing churches today, and, finally, some insight into how to expand your ministry potential by approaching your leadership and involvement in the church in new ways. These principles are biblical and practical.

Before continuing, I would like to take a moment to acknowledge those who have helped to make this book a possibility. First, I want to acknowledge the people of Salem Covenant Church for their willingness to take risks, to experiment with new ideas, and to share in church life and ministry together. Without their support and participation, many of the ideas presented in this book may have never been given the opportunity to exist. I also want to acknowledge my wife Carolyn Bixby, Dorine Boesel, and my pastoral colleagues David Chandler, Mark Torgerson, Andrew Newlin, and Cheryl Anderson for the support they gave me as I wrote and edited this book. Also, I would like to acknowledge the general support that I have received in life and ministry from those who have been my ministry mentors: The Reverends Dennis Moon, Isolde Anderson, Timothy Heintzelman, Richard Sears, and all the ministers, past and present, who have been involved with my ministers' support group. Many individuals have also helped me with the publishing process: Rob Johnston, Clay Winters, Jim Hawkinson, and Brad Bergfalk. I would also like to acknowledge my professors and classmates from North Park Theological Seminary and Hope College. In addition, I would like to acknowledge Kim Sadler and the people at the Pilgrim Press for believing in this book and for the support they have offered me. Further, I would like to acknowledge and thank George B. Thompson Jr. for writing the foreword. Finally, I offer special thanks to my family for their support: my parents Jim and Karen Bixby; my siblings Todd, Bob, and Jennifer; their families; and my two daughters, Katie and Kiersten.

Introduction

The church monster is the extensive conflict, anxiety, and bureaucracy that grows out of poor structure and the inability to make decisions effectively and efficiently. What was once a church mouse, a small irritating pest, is now a church monster—a huge, devastating problem. Churches are having a hard time surviving, let alone thriving, in the midst of all this conflict and anxiety. And the overgrown, complicated church structures we have developed in the past not only feed into this, they also keep our churches from establishing the kind of momentum they need to survive and thrive in the present age. These complicated systems stifle progress and keep pastors and churches preoccupied with their administrative nightmares.

The impact of the church monster on our churches can be seen in the number of pastors leaving their churches or who are being asked to leave their churches prematurely because of conflicts that have arisen between them and a few individuals in their congregations. These conflicts range from the color of carpeting to doctrinal differences. They may be related to ministry opportunities, worship style, program choices, wallpaper, or which way the toilet paper should hang off the roll in the church bathrooms. Whatever the issue, it often seems that a few individuals are given enough power to get rid of their pastors or to make life within their church so miserable that these pastors want to leave.

The problem is not that pastors are leaving. The problem is that pastors leave prematurely because of the unrequested, undesirable influence of a few individuals. And congregations often feel powerless in these situations. Churches are falling apart because they do not know how to handle conflicts or how to respond to their failure in the midst of these situations. Therefore, churches split and disintegrate. At times, pastors and church leaders blame their area ministers or conference superintendents, but more often than not, these individuals are in no better a position to resolve conflicts than are pastors and local church leaders. Therefore, churches must be equipped to deal appropriately with conflict as it arises.

In previous generations, churches had the luxury of not having to worry as much about tension and conflict. People attended and stayed at local churches out of a sense of denominational identity and loyalty. People saw themselves as Lutherans, Methodists, Catholics, Presbyterians, Baptists, Congregationalists, Covenanters, or Episcopalians. And often, church membership was tied together with family identity. Conflicts that went on behind the scenes did not have the same kind of impact that they have today. People no longer attend churches out of a pure sense of loyalty or obligation. They attend because they want to participate in their worship and ministries.

In his book *Evangelism that Works*, George Barna, founder and president of Barna Research Group, writes, "Perhaps four or five decades ago people would grit their teeth and bear an unsatisfying or unfulfilling church experience. Today, however, we are liberated from traditions, loyalties, commitments, and social expectations. It's every person for himself or herself. Whichever life options are readily available to the person and promise the most appealing and pleasing set of outcomes will win the momentary allegiance of the typical adult, regardless of the long-term consequences or effects of their choices."[1]

People inside the church today may have an increased level of tolerance for the conflict existing within their congregations. But people outside the church, looking in, have little, if any, tolerance or understanding of this type of anxiety within the congregations they visit. The monster keeps new people from coming in and tenured people from believing that things can change.

Barna writes, "Eighty-five percent of all nonchurched adults have had a prolonged period of time during which they consistently attended a church or religious center. Few adults living in America today have never had a serious and protracted church experience. What makes this realization so powerful is that adults attend church of their own volition. For people to leave, they often must be driven away."[2]

Barna continues saying, "Before we can hope to attract the dechurched, we must address the past shortcomings they have experienced and move them beyond those concerns toward a more fulfilling and useful relationship with God and his people."[3]

The existence of the church monster is the reason there are so many "de-churched" people in our society. And if churches do not find ways to contend with it, the monster will continue on its destructive path. To survive and thrive in this day and age, we must present a viable challenge that will transform this monster back into a mouse.

We may never be able to rid ourselves of conflict altogether, but we can contain it and limit its power. Our goal must be to get back to a place where God's truth has more of an impact on our churches than does the anxiety that has become so prevalent in churches today.

The existence of the monster is also the reason so many people in our society say they do not believe in "organized religion." People are often fed up with and disenchanted by an overly organized, institutional approach to "being the church." When people say they do not believe in "organized religion," they are not saying they want to be a part of disorganized churches. They would prefer less-organized churches. People are tired of churches that seem more focused on meetings than ministry and more focused on conflict than community. This is why we must "speak the truth in love," and why we must "grow up in every way into him who is the head, into Christ." (Eph 4:15)

Part 1
RESTRUCTURING

1

The Anxiety Frenzy

I was right out of seminary and in my first few months of pastoral ministry when the stove issue hit. A man in our church had been offered an industrial gas stove that had been taken out of a local restaurant. He thought it could be used to replace the ordinary electric stoves in our church kitchen. Little did he realize this would create a major rift within our congregation between those who preferred gas stoves and those who preferred electric. I was not the least bit concerned about which type of stove we had in our kitchen, so I figured I would stay as far away from this issue as I could. Nevertheless, I was stunned by the amount of time and energy consumed by people fighting about this issue in our church. Every time I turned around, people seemed to be talking about it, and no one seemed to know how to resolve the matter. The anxiety level was enormous, and yet I had no idea why. What kind of stove we had in our kitchen seemed so far removed from the central mission of our church, and yet people were allowing the issue to tear us apart.

WASTING TIME AND ENERGY

Imagine if you were to take all the time and energy wasted on conflicts in your church and use it for mission and ministry. Your church could do amazing things to expand the impact of the body of Christ in our communities and our world. 1 Peter 4:10 says, "Like good stewards of the manifold grace of God, serve one another with whatever gift each of you has received." This text calls us to use our time and energy effectively for God's purposes. God does not want us to waste our time and energy feeding the anxiety monster. Neither do our people. The tendency for pastors is to blame this anxiety frenzy on people's pettiness. However, deep down, the people of our churches want to be good stewards of their time and energy. They want the time and energy they offer to the church to be used effectively in accordance with God's principles and priorities. They do not want to use their time and energy to feed the anxiety monster, and yet many people find themselves unintentionally doing it.

The people involved with the stove issue in our church were not pleased with the amount of time and energy they were spending on this issue. It disgusted and frustrated them, and yet many of them still had strong, clearly defined opinions about whether or not we should use gas or electric in our kitchen. The problem is not that people have opinions on these matters. The problem is that most churches are not set up to make decisions like this effectively or efficiently. Most churches are structured in a way that actually prevents decisions from ever being made. Thus, churches become paralyzed and polarized by questions that seem so far removed from the central mission of the church.

The problem is not bad people. The problem is bad church structure. In relationship to the stove issue, the problem was not that the people at Salem Covenant Church were not spiritual or mission-minded enough. The problem was they were trying to function in a system that was keeping them from being able to make decisions in an expeditious manner. They did not know where to turn to resolve the issue. This is why such a peripheral issue could become a central problem, and why the anxiety created in situations like these surprises and discourages pastors and laypeople alike.

UNITY AND DIVERSITY

Diversity, though desired, can bring with it many challenges to a church. As individuals, we all have different personalities, backgrounds, maturity levels, passions, and interests. It is no wonder churches have a hard time making decisions. Nevertheless, we are called to be unified within the church. In 1 Corinthians 1:10 the apostle Paul says, "I appeal to you, brothers and sisters, by the name of our Lord Jesus Christ, that all of you be in agreement and that there be no divisions among you, but that you be united in the same mind and the same purpose." Deep down, I believe that we are already united in the same mind and purpose as disciples through our belief in Jesus Christ.

The difficulty is in making practical decisions effectively and efficiently in the midst of the diversity of opinions and personalities that exist in our congregations. The things that typically divide us are secondary to the core beliefs and values we share and the core issues we face as Christians. The structure of our churches should help us to effectively manage ministry in the midst of our diversity. Church systems should provide us with a means for making decisions without disrupting the community and the ministry that is taking place. Jesus Christ is the great unifier, and yet it is only in the midst of diversity that our unity in Christ means anything.

In his first letter to the Corinthians, the apostle Paul wrote,

> For just as the body is one and has many members, and all the members of the body, though many, are one body, so it is with Christ. For in the one Spirit we were all baptized into one body—Jews or Greeks, slaves or free—and we were all made to drink of one Spirit. Indeed, the body does not consist of one member but of many. If the foot would say, "Because I am not a hand, I do not belong to the body," that would not make it any less a part of the body. And if the ear would say, "Because I am not an eye, I do not belong to the body," that would not make it any less a part of the body. If the whole body were an eye, where would the hearing be? If the whole body were hearing, where would the sense of smell be? (1 Cor 12:12–17)

Paul makes it clear through this passage that unity is something that can be found in the midst of our diversity and that it is more meaningful and powerful because of our diversity. According to Paul, unity within our churches ought to be one of our top priorities, and yet congregations in our society are experiencing extremely low levels of unity and extremely high levels of disharmony. Churches are falling apart because they do not know how to function effectively within their current systems. And although there are many reasons why so many congregations are experiencing so much disharmony in this day and age, the primary reason is because congregations have been structured for frustration, and people are no longer tolerant of things that waste their time.

In his book *Dancing with Dinosaurs*, highly respected author and church consultant William Easum writes, "In the emerging society, leaders will be those willing to risk leaving the safety of the 'good-ole-boy" system. Those who remain tied to bureaucracy will be lost. Institutions that cling to their bureaucracies will vanish."[1]

Easum continues, "The twenty-first century will be an exciting time for ministry. Pastors who are secure enough to risk and venture into uncharted waters will do well. They will create a variety of new ministries that reach a variety of new needs and hurts."[2]

HAND HOLDING AND FIRE FIGHTING

Most pastors I know are tired of tending to fires started by those who call themselves church leaders, and they are overburdened by the amount of hand-holding and refereeing they have to do within their congregations. People do not enter into full-time ministry to become babysitters and police officers. They enter into full-time ministry hoping to become transformational leaders who help lead people to Christ and to participate in the redemptive ministry of their churches. Too many pastors feel their congregations waste their time and energy, and, ironically, the members of these same congregations feel like their time and energy is being wasted by their pastors. Pastors and lay leaders alike often feel like pinballs in a giant pinball machine. We keep getting knocked around, but we never seem to get anywhere. The anxiety monster keeps getting bigger and bigger, and we keep feeding it more of what it wants. We give life to this monster, and, in return, it sucks the life out of our churches and out of us.

Pastors are not only frustrated by the amount of fire fighting and hand-holding required, they are also frustrated by the way specific individuals seem to be allowed to frustrate the system and to set up roadblocks for every new initiative, even if it is supported by the majority of the congregation. In these circumstances, individual leaders do not have enough power to make practical day-to-day decisions, and yet too many individuals seem to have more than enough power to keep big decisions from being made. This is why it takes so much time for decisions to be made in most churches and why people feel like their churches are too preoccupied with conflict.

In his book *Well-Intentioned Dragons*, Marshall Shelly, editor of *Leadership Journal*, begins by writing about the people in our churches who seem to enjoy creating conflict. After generally describing these "well-intentioned dragons," Shelly writes about our best defense saying,

> Landscapers know the best way to prevent weeds is not to attack them individually. Uprooting stubborn dandelions or chickweed one by one will improve appearances temporarily, but within days, the troublesome plants will be back. The best way to handle weeds is a thick, healthy lawn, which keeps them from springing up in the first place.[3]

The goal in challenging the church monster is to help our people become better equipped for mission and ministry. The goal is to function more effectively and efficiently so that well-managed ministries keep problematic people and situations from disrupting their mission and ministries. In a properly structured church, "well-intentioned dragons" are ministered to but not given permission to get in the way of the other ministry that is taking place. The monster can be contained and its power can be limited.

The Overly Organized Church

In a laundry-detergent commercial a few years ago, a woman spoke about her occupation as an owner and operator of a bed and breakfast saying, "It takes a lot of work to make it seem like it runs itself." In many ways, church leaders should be able to say the same thing about their roles within their churches. The focus within our churches should not be on church government and decision-making, but rather on mission and ministry. Our churches need to be set up so that a few people should be able to work hard to do all the behind-the-scenes work. It should be seen as a small part of all we do.

Marshall Shelly writes, "In the church, administrative details and paperwork are necessary. After all, someone must decide who's going to mow the church lawn, what color to paint the nursery, and whom we can get to serve on the social committee. But a church overloaded with bureaucratic ministries is a prime target for a dragon attack."[1]

MALIGNANT MISTRUST

Trust neutralizes tension and contention. Most church structures, however, breed malignant mistrust. They are set up in such a way that trust is easily broken, and mistrust acts as an inhibitor to mission and ministry. Mistrust is disruptive to the development of both ministry and community. It is malignant in the sense that it can be terminal. It is like cancer in that it is hard to see, but it is extremely destructive. Mistrust is the cancer within our churches, and the conflicts that arise because of this mistrust are the visible tumors.

We can all come up with a million and one reasons why mistrust exists in our particular churches. It is easy to point fingers and create scapegoats, but all we really do is identify the symptoms of more systemic problems. Systematically, most churches today have been set up for disaster, and when disaster strikes, everyone struggles to find someone to blame. The blame often falls on the pastor. Some churches go through pastors every two to three years because of the "blame game." And some churches, after a long series of short-term pastorates, start to blame themselves and think of themselves as sick or dysfunctional; however, these diagnoses are often used as excuses for bad behavior rather than as a starting point toward real solutions.

The primary problem is not with the people or their pastors, but with the church structure and system. All churches have a certain amount of sickness and a certain number of sick people. The key is developing a system that enables you to function in the midst of the diversity, sin, and sickness that exists in your congregation. Churches are not sick or healthy, but well structured or poorly structured. A well-structured church will keep the sick people we are serving from disrupting our ministries. Good structure will keep sick people from being in the center of your church government. These "sick people" are coming to the church to be helped, not hurt. It is our responsibility as leaders to make sure they are not the next victims of the church monster.

In Romans 14:13–19, the apostle Paul says,

> Let us therefore no longer pass judgment on one another, but resolve instead never to put a stumbling block or hindrance in the way of another. I know and am persuaded in the Lord Jesus that nothing is unclean in itself; but it is unclean for anyone who thinks it unclean. If your brother or sister is being injured by what you eat, you are no longer walking in love. Do not let what you eat cause the ruin of one for whom Christ died. So do not let your good be spoken of as evil. For the Kingdom of God is not food and drink but righteousness and peace and joy in the Holy Spirit. The one who thus serves Christ is acceptable to God and has human approval. Let us then pursue what makes for peace and for mutual up-building.

The complicated structure in so many of our churches is often a stumbling block and a hindrance to some on a spiritual level, particularly those who are spiritually weak. Therefore, those of us who are mature in the faith need to be responsible for the way that our churches function. We need to make sure people are not injured by the way we do things organizationally. We need to make sure we are "walking in love" in our ministries and that our "good" is not being "spoken of as evil." It is essential we pursue that which "makes for peace and for mutual up-building."

Mistrust and Change

Mistrust leads churches to establish too much structure, which in turn leads to too much chaos and confusion. We have developed complex systems of checks and balances that keep decisions from being made too quickly, if at all. These systems have been built on a lack of trust in the individuals and small groups called on to make major decisions for their churches. Often, this gives other individuals the power to keep decisions from being made. Therefore, the structural chaos so many churches are experiencing serves a very specific purpose in these overgrown systems of mistrust. The purpose is to keep things from changing. The problem is, this also keeps churches from ministering. It keeps the monster alive and limits the impact of our churches.

Congregations fear change, and when systems are not in place to guard against excessive change, people take it upon themselves to ensure it does not happen at all. This is why very little trust develops within these systems and why very little gets accomplished despite all the time and energy people put into their churches. Lay leaders and pastors are left frustrated, because they end up bearing a lot of responsibility without being given any real authority. Momentum rarely develops, and individual leaders rarely feel like they are having an impact. Most feel they are simply spinning their wheels.

Marshall Shelly writes, "Unemployment will breed discontentment, whether in Pennsylvania steel towns, urban ghettos, or the church. Those fully employed in significant ministry are less likely to become troublesome."[2]

Shelly also writes, "Some of the most significant ministry is not done inside the walls of the church, but outside, where the gospel has its most visible effect."[3] The people in our churches need to be employed in real-life, active ministry, not in complicated and unnecessary bureaucracy.

Overgrown Church Governments

Kennon Callahan is a nationally recognized church consultant who specializes in church planning. In his book, *Twelve Keys to an Effective Church*, one "key" to effectiveness that he identifies is "Streamlined Structure and Solid Participatory Decision Making." Callahan writes,

A streamlined organizational structure facilitates the straightforward development, deployment, and delegation of responsibilities, authority, and accountability so that effective accomplishments and achievements can occur.[4]

Earlier in the same chapter, Callahan argues, "Years ago, the myth was spawned that the way to involve people is to put them on a committee, and the results of this myth have been among the most harmful and destructive factors to many congregations' status as declining or dying churches."[5]

Top-heavy, overgrown church governments are the guardians of mistrust in congregational systems. Overgrown church governments exist because of mistrust, and mistrust exists because of overgrown church governments. Many established churches have become so top-heavy that the people in these churches just barely feel a part of their congregations. Overly organized churches are inflexible and immovable. People become so accustomed to living in an environment where trust does not exist that they are unaware of the burden it places on their churches. This is why it is hard for churches to understand why certain positive things do not happen and why certain negative things keep on happening.

In Matthew 6:25–33, Jesus said,

> Therefore, I tell you, do not worry about your life, what you will eat or what you will drink, or about your body, what you will wear. Is not life more than food, and the body more than clothing? Look at the birds of the air; they neither sow nor reap nor gather into barns, and yet your heavenly Father feeds them. Are you not of more value than they? And can any of you by worrying add a single hour to your span of life? And why do you worry about clothing? Consider the lilies of the field, how they grow; they neither toil nor spin, yet I tell you, even Solomon in all his glory was not clothed like one of these. But if God so clothes the grass of the field, which is alive today and tomorrow is thrown into the oven, will he not much more clothe you—you of little faith? Therefore do not worry, saying, "What will we eat?" or "What will we drink?" or "What will we wear?" For it is the Gentiles who strive for all these things; and indeed your heavenly Father knows that you need all these things. But strive first for the dominion of

God and his righteousness, and all these things will be given to you as well.

There is too much worry in our churches today, and often we worry unnecessarily about insignificant things. We have too little faith and not nearly enough faithfulness. Jesus calls us in the above passage to "strive first for the dominion of God and his righteousness." All these other things will be given to us as well.

Churches must discover ways to minimize their church governments while simultaneously maximizing their potential for active ministry. We all need to develop ways to shift our focus off meetings and onto ministry, off conflict and onto community. But how do we do this when the anxiety monster seems to be setting the agenda? How do we do this when everything going on in our churches seems beyond our control?

Thomas Bandy is the program officer of congregational mission and evangelism for the United Church of Canada and a leader in the field of congregational intervention. In his book *Moving Off the Map*, Bandy writes, "Church transformation is a matter of systemic change, not mere programmatic change. The whole system of congregational life and mission, the ebb and flow of both spontaneous and intentional activity, must ultimately be changed."[6]

The key to developing a successful ministry is to get the people of your church excited about being involved with your ministries. With regard to church structure, we need to make sure that our systems are not keeping people from participating in our ministries. Simplifying our systems makes them more manageable. Systems should help us function better, not hinder us. We need to make sure that our systems are not getting in the way of what God is trying to accomplish through us and for us. Top-heavy, overgrown church governments have a tendency to get in the way of a lot of things. This is why downsizing and centralizing our church governments makes so much sense. It is also why I believe that a radical commitment to congregational decision-making makes sense. These two principles can help our churches to function better and to minister more freely and creatively.

Downsizing and Centralizing

When Salem Covenant Church first contacted me while I was still in seminary about the possibility of serving as their pastor, they sent me a church profile. In the profile, I observed that there were twenty-eight people on their central board and between thirty-five and forty people attending worship regularly. I could not understand why such a large percentage of the church was involved with the running of this small congregation. I was glad to discover at a later date that during their interim period the church switched to a church-council system, where the chair of each board sat on the council and the other members of each board met only when necessary. At the time, the church council consisted of ten people, and, when I arrived, we quickly discovered that it was not necessary for any of these other boards to meet regularly. Our downsized and centralized church government evolved as our board system disintegrated.

DOWNSIZING

Downsizing is simple. You eliminate all your boards, like your board of deacons, board of trustees, and board of Christian education, and create individual leadership positions on one centralized church council. The primary problem with having several administrative boards is that these boards have too much time on their hands and too few substantive issues on their agendas. If you centralize your church government and eliminate all other administrative bodies, your meetings will be filled with important agenda items and a clear sense of purpose and accomplishment. Most people feel good about being a part of an administrative body that makes significant decisions and helps to manage a significant amount of ministry. This is why shrinking and centralizing is so beneficial.

Smaller governing bodies also allow for more freedom and flexibility within churches. Freedom and flexibility allows individuals to minister creatively and to use their time and energy effectively and efficiently. Doing away with unnecessary bureaucracy will help churches accomplish this. Most churches should be able to downsize and centralize their church governments into one group of eight to ten people, including the pastor, who will be an *ex-officio* member. The average sized church in the United States is under 150 people.[1] Thus, most churches should be able to operate effectively with one, centralized, church-governing body.

If you are going to downsize and centralize your church government, there should be one group of no more than twelve people charged with the task of overseeing your ministries. If you are in a church of less than 150 people, you should have a group of no more than eight to twelve people serving as your church council. Bigger churches should limit their council to twelve people, but should use ten to fifteen percent of their people on ministry teams that will help to manage their ministries effectively under the direction of the church council. These ministry teams should be seen as interdependent agents of the church council. There is no need to have a member of each ministry team on the church council or to have council members chair these ministry teams. However, someone should be identified as a liaison to each of the ministry teams, and they should recognize that they are ultimately accountable to the council and congregation.

Any sized church can use individuals, pairs, or small groups of people to organize and implement ministries approved by the church council or the congregation. Smaller churches do not need ministry teams; they need coordinators or managers of their ministries. Individual leaders tend to be very effective at managing ministries if they are given the authority to do so. Therefore, your church council should not only be charged with the task of overseeing the ministries, but also with the task of delegating authority for the implementation of these ministries. Most churches have very capable people who are willing to lead. The problem is they never get asked. They only get asked to be on stagnant boards that do very little in terms of leadership.

Churches must begin to see individuals as potential leaders and each member as a potential participant in their ministries. Each person on your church council should be seen as an individual leader and should be responsible for some area in the life of the church. For example, at Salem we have a chairperson, a vice chairperson, secretary, treasurer, Christian-education coordinator, a trustee coordinator, a diaconate coordinator, and an outreach coordinator. We also hold a philosophy that states that every member of our church is a deacon, a trustee, a Christian-educator, and an outreach minister. The point is that every member feels some responsibility for the spiritual care of the people in our congregation, for the practical care of our grounds and facilities, for the activities of our Christian education and discipleship efforts, and for helping our church to reach out beyond our walls.

Ephesians 4:11–13 states,

> The gifts he gave were that some would be apostles, some prophets, some evangelists, some pastors and teachers, to equip the saints for the work of ministry, for building up the body of Christ, until all of us come to the unity of faith and of the knowledge of the Son of God, to maturity, to the measure of the full stature of Christ.

We should not deny our differences. We are not all called to fulfill the same roles and responsibilities; and yet we are supposed to discern our spiritual gifts and take advantage of our differences to help the church accomplish more for Jesus Christ through our mission and ministries. There is a core set of responsibilities associated with any congregation that the membership ought to fulfill. You do not need the gift of evangelism to invite a neighbor to worship, the gift of hospitality to bring apple juice to Vacation Bible School, or the gift of generosity to be a good steward of your income. This is why we should all see ourselves as deacons, trustees, Christian-educators, and outreach ministers. If we all came to believe and live this as church members, it would make most of our boards and committees radically unnecessary.

In *The Purpose-Driven Church,* Rick Warren, senior pastor of Saddleback Valley Community Church in Orange County, California, writes, "I've always loved Elton Trueblood's name for the church: 'The Company of the Committed.' It would be wonderful if every church was known for the commitment of its members. Unfortunately, churches are often held together by committees rather than commitment."[2]

PARTICIPATION IN MINISTRY

One of my core beliefs is that people would rather participate in church ministry than in church administration. Many people even avoid getting involved with church ministries because they are afraid they are going to get pulled onto a board or sucked into the bureaucracy of their local churches. They avoid even what they would love to do because they are afraid of being stuck doing things they really do not enjoy doing. This dynamic stifles the potential our churches have for building excitement and enthusiasm into our ministries. Smaller church governments can help free people up to participate in ministry without the threat of being pulled onto a board or forced into a committee.

The church is not an institution, it is a people. Therefore, we need people to participate in the life and ministries of our local churches more than we need them to serve in administration and oversight. The people are the church, not just the leaders.

1 Peter 2:4–5 says, "Come to him, a living stone, though rejected by mortals yet chosen and precious in God's sight, and like living stones, let yourselves be built into a spiritual house, to be a holy priesthood, to offer spiritual sacrifices acceptable to God through Jesus Christ."

Allowing yourself to be placed on a governing board is not the same thing as allowing yourself to be "built into a spiritual house." The diaconate coordinator at Salem Covenant Church is responsible for making sure communion is organized on the first Sunday of every month. She has four people who take turns setting up communion and finding other church members to help serve communion on those days. Since every member at Salem Covenant Church is considered a deacon, any member can serve communion on any given Sunday. Thus, we have a wide range of people who participate in this side of our ministries. It is not uncommon to see a new member serve communion on a Sunday morning in our church.

Too much bureaucracy or too many administrative boards end up isolating people into particular areas of involvement within the life of the church. People end up narrowing their focus to a single area of concern, such as Christian education, building and grounds, worship and care, or mission and outreach. Not only are people split up and divided between different areas of responsibility, but also competing agendas develop, and they fight over resources. Therefore, these administrative boards not only end up feeling restrictive and confining but also competitive and undervalued. They compare themselves to each other and are left constantly wondering which of them is most important.

When you centralize your church government, there is a common sense of mission: One vision, one set of priorities, and one group empowered by your congregation to be responsible for the congregation's stewardship of its resources. It ends up being reflective of Ephesians 4:4–5, where it says, "There is one body and one Spirit, just as you were called to the one hope of your calling, one Lord, one faith, one baptism, one God and Father of all, who is above all and through all and in all."

This concept of "oneness" and being of the "same mind and purpose" is taken a step further in Philippians 2:4, when the apostle Paul says, "Let the same mind be in you that was in Christ Jesus." We are all called to be of the same mind as Jesus. In other words, we must develop thinking patterns that resemble his. We must develop hearts that have the same kind of passion and compassion he had.

In his book *Maximize Your Ministry*, Robert Slocum, a Presbyterian lay leader and business person, writes, "I am convinced the effective church for the twenty-first century will be the church that mobilizes, equips, empowers, and supports ordinary Christians in ministry. We must devise and put into practice a new strategy for making ordinary Christians effective in both the Church Gathered and the Church Scattered."[3]

Slocum also writes, "The 'great, great' churches will be those that serve as training camps for lay men and women who hear Christ call them to climb their particular mountain and who respond to the call."[4]

People in a downsized and centralized church-system are freed up to become true disciples of Jesus. Less-organized churches become effective alternatives to overly organized religious institutions. The freedom and flexibility that evolves from being effectively less organized allows for creativity and energy to develop in church ministries. People begin to think in terms of possibilities and opportunities rather than responsibilities and obligations. This kind of participation in ministry ends up being life-affirming and God-honoring for most people.

PEOPLE AND LEADERSHIP

Those who serve on a downsized and centralized church council are typically going to be very busy people in the life of the church. Not only do they attend meetings and lead in their particular areas of the church, they also participate in a variety of other areas in the life of the church. They do a lot. However, the good news is that they also receive a lot of recognition and appreciation for their work. Their time is appreciated, and their accomplishments celebrated. These leaders feel like their time and talents are being used more effectively and efficiently, and so do their pastors.

Downsizing and centralizing your church government not only helps individual leaders feel as though their time and energy are being used more effectively, individuals participating in the church's ministries feel the same sense of purpose and meaning. The key is finding people who have the spiritual gifts of administration and leadership to be on your church council, and then to let everyone else serve in the capacities to which they feel called and led.

Greg Laurie, speaking about his role as the pastor of a very large church in his book *The Upside-Down Church*, says, "I try not to micromanage but rather to enable and encourage the others in the calling God has put on their lives." Laurie continues, "I have been practicing this approach from the very beginning of our ministry, trying to identify the gifts of people and then turning those people loose where they can make the greatest difference."[5]

The glory in all of this is that people end up using their spiritual gifts in accordance with their personal passions and the specific needs of your church and community. More people are engaged in meaningful ministry and fewer in meaningless meetings.

In his book *Unleashing the Church*, Frank Tillapaugh, pastor of Bear Valley Baptist Church, distinguishes between "church work" and doing "the work of the church." In a chapter entitled "Unleashing the Laity," he refers to a navigator conference he once attended. Tillapaugh writes,

At a Navigator conference years ago the main speaker referred to what he termed 'front-line' and 'rear-echelon' ministries. As a combat veteran he had vivid memories of the difference in attitude between those directly joined in battle on the front lines and those indirectly involved a few miles behind in the rear echelon. The guys on the front line didn't complain much. They were too busy fighting the enemy. . . . Once you went a few miles behind the front, however, attitudes changed drastically. Back there, griping was a way of life. Men complained about everything—the food, the weather, the officers. Something was wrong with everyone and everything.[6]

The exciting thing about smaller, centralized church governments is that you have fewer people involved in "rear echelon" ministries and more people involved with "front line" ministries. The ones in the "rear echelon" are also so busy that they do not have time to create problems, and they spend enough time on the "front lines" to know these activities are our top priorities.

A Radical Commitment

Let me return to the "stove issue." Once I realized the stove issue at Salem Covenant Church would not disappear, I quickly realized that we needed to have a congregational meeting to make a decision and move into the future without this issue hanging over our heads. We organized what I affectionately refer to as "The Stove Meeting." I ended up running this meeting because I was far more impartial on the issue than our chairperson. I called everyone together and asked them to list the positives and negatives of gas verses electric stoves. We then went on a little field trip to the shed where this stove was being stored. As it turned out, the stove was not in very good condition. We returned to the room where we were having this meeting and voted on paper ballots. I was then able to say that whatever the decision, once it was made, the issue must be put behind us. The decision was clear, and we never heard about it again.

THE STOVE MEETING

Through the stove meeting, we figured out there are ways to deal with conflicts and to make difficult decisions in a fair and open manner. You could almost hear a sigh of relief from our congregation after the meeting. People were openly relieved to know a mechanism was in place to deal with conflicts and make these kinds of decisions quickly and cooperatively. This meeting not only kept a few individuals from making this decision for the whole congregation, it also kept the decision from becoming a bigger deal than it needed to be. Sure, there were people who did not like the outcome. However, once the decision was made in a fair and open manner, we were able to get on with mission and ministry. Those in disagreement recognized this decision was not closely related to the central mission of our church. Thus, once a decision was made, they could easily get on with their lives, and the church as a whole could get on with its ministries.

This approach to congregational discernment allows everyone to express their opinions, and yet there is no way to guarantee that any one person will get their way. Most people are mature enough to accept group decisions as long as they have an equal opportunity to speak out and to vote on the matter. Each member has one voice and one vote in a democratic congregational system. As I mentioned before, I never had the sense that "the stove issue" became such a big deal because our people were not mission-minded or spiritual enough. My sense was they were being held back by an inability to make decisions in an effective and efficient manner. The stove issue helped us to realize the value of making a radical commitment to congregational decision-making.

One of the fears pastors and other church leaders express with this approach to making decisions has to do with the number of petty things that they imagine will come before their congregations. But, often, the number of the petty things that come up shrinks dramatically with this kind of approach. Our Council leaders have become quite comfortable with referring significant decisions to the congregation and very good at discerning which things the congregation does and does not need to handle. We have quarterly, congregational meetings and occasionally call for special meetings about specific issues. We do not meet congregationally more often than we did in the past, but we do more in these meetings. People are now less preoccupied with the process and more focused on making decisions that help to support our mission and ministries.

We may not always get our way in this type of system, but we will be more focused on discerning God's will and ways because of it. In Colossians 3:12–17, the apostle Paul writes,

> As God's chosen ones, holy and beloved, clothe yourselves with compassion, kindness, humility, meekness, and patience. Bear with one another and, if anyone has a complaint against another, forgive each other; just as the Lord has forgiven you, so you also must forgive. Above all, clothe yourselves with love, which binds everything together in perfect harmony. And let the peace of Christ rule in your hearts, to which indeed you were called in the one body. And be thankful. Let the word of Christ dwell in

you richly; teach and admonish one another in all wisdom; and with gratitude in your hearts sing psalms, hymns, and spiritual songs to God. And whatever you do, in word or deed, do everything in the name of the Lord Jesus, giving thanks to God the Father through him.

THE PROCESS

Most church conflict has to do with how decisions are made, not what decisions are made. People do not like being excluded from the process when a decision matters to them. Thus, the color of the carpeting in the fellowship hall may not seem like a major decision with regard to our mission and ministries, but it is a major decision in the minds of those who care about the color of the carpeting. They will live with whatever decision gets made, but they will have a difficult time living with any decision made in a process that completely excludes them and their opinions. Often, there are too many people involved with the day-to-day decisions in a church and not enough people involved with major and potentially controversial decisions.

To develop a radical commitment to making decisions congregationally, we have to learn to trust the collective wisdom of our congregations. This sounds simple, but how do we do this with a diverse group of people who we cannot be sure will have the same intentions and opinions as ourselves? How can we be sure, or make sure, others will want the same kind of stove we want in our church kitchens or the same color carpeting we want in our sanctuaries? Ultimately, we cannot. However, this is where a radical commitment to making decisions congregationally is essential.

In Philippians 2:2–4, the apostle Paul says, "Make my joy complete: be of the same mind, having the same love, being in full accord and of one mind. Do nothing from selfish ambition or conceit, but in humility regard others as better than yourselves. Let each of you look not to your own interests, but to the interests of others."

This type of democratic process may not seem spiritual within the context of *Robert's Rules of Order* and formal agendas. However, within the context of a congregation, democratic decision-making does call on us to surrender control and to put our trust in each other and God.

We may not get our way every time a decision is made, but we can be confident that decisions are being made fairly and openly and that decisions with significance in God's eyes are being made with the guidance of the Holy Spirit.

DEVELOPING TRUST

Authentic discernment helps the members of our churches develop a sense of ownership in relationship to our mission and ministries. It also encourages an atmosphere of trust. If pastors and lay leaders constantly try to sneak significant decisions through their committees, boards, or commissions, congregations begin to mistrust their pastors and leaders. A radical commitment to democratic congregational decision-making eliminates the need for the excessive bureaucracy and the systems of checks and balances that exist in most of our congregations. This trust also makes downsizing our church governments relatively easy. Reliance on the congregation for making decisions enables the church to feel that there is a system in place that will keep things from changing too rapidly.

Kennon Callahan, in *Twelve Keys to an Effective Church,* states, "Congregations that have a cumbersome decision-making process will be likely to have a complex organizational structure. By the same token, their complex organizational structure will contribute directly to the cumbersomeness of the decision-making process."[1]

All this boils down to the fact that we need to simplify our systems and to work hard at keeping things simple and straightforward within our systems.

Callahan writes, "Insofar as a congregation has a streamlined structure and solid, participatory decision making, that congregation is likely to move forward with confidence and competence in the direction that will best put in place its solid destiny as a missional church."[2]

Small, centralized church governments may sound scary to some congregations because it seems to place a lot of power in the hands of a few. However, if a group of leaders is radically committed to these democratic principles, the congregation will trust this group of ten or so individuals to bring any major decisions before them. The general rule of thumb at Salem Covenant Church is that any decision that seems potentially controversial or anxiety producing should be brought before the congregation. This includes issues that are centrally related to our mission and peripheral matters. The key is discerning which issues are sufficiently important to enough people to make it worth bringing before the congregation, keeping in mind that what is unimportant to some people is very important to others. If there is any question in the minds of church leaders as to whether or not to bring something before the congregation, we do so.

Most individual leaders seem to prefer this type of process. They see their congregation as a great resource rather than a last resort, and they feel safer making significant decisions with the congregation's approval and backing. Individual leaders need a certain amount of authority. However, they do not want too much authority because of the responsibility that goes with it. What leaders ultimately need is trust, not control. Trust allows pastors and other individual leaders to have a lot of influence within their churches. Mistrust develops when pastors and individual leaders try to make major decisions without consulting their congregations.

I often hear about situations where pastors push decisions through their boards. Quite often, these are decisions that pastors do not think their congregations would approve if asked. This is where trust gets broken. The people on these administrative boards end up feeling used by their pastor, and the people in the church end up feeling violated by this misuse of power and authority. The people in our congregations not only want quality decisions to be made, they also want these decisions to be made in a high-quality manner.

PROPOSALS AND POWER STRUGGLES

A commitment to making major decisions together not only prevents individuals from having too much authority, it ensures that individual leaders have enough authority to make practical day-to-day decisions. Congregations do not want to be bothered with day-to-day decisions that can be handled by people in leadership positions. If a toilet is broken and needs to be fixed, the congregation does not need to be consulted about whether or not to contact a plumber. However, if leaders want to renovate the sanctuary and select a new color of carpeting, it would be wise to get congregational approval for both the general proposal and the specific plans.

Turning to the congregation as a last resort leaves too much room for power struggles. Church leaders often come up with good ideas and create committees. These committees then spend huge amounts of time and energy putting together plans. These committees then go to the congregation, only to be frustrated by a rejection of the general proposal. Within this new type of system, you can take a general proposal to the congregation first and have them approve the idea before the specific plans are made. Once the general idea is approved, then you form a committee to do the detailed work of putting the plan together, and you later seek to approve the final plans at another congregational meeting.

This way, the process is streamlined, and authority is used appropriately and held in proper perspective. It gives the congregation the right to say no to the general idea without making committee members feel as though their work was unappreciated or a waste of their time. At the same time, it keeps committee members from feeling they are entitled to a yes vote simply because they have given a great deal of time and energy to a project. If you approve the idea first, you enable the church to develop a sense of ownership in the project before all the time and energy is put into developing the specific plans for the final proposal.

Let me share a major decision Salem Covenant Church recently made with regard to youth ministry at our church. The idea of hiring our first full-time youth pastor was suggested one week prior to our annual meeting in January 2000. We put it on the agenda, and it was discussed. There seemed to be a positive sense about it. A committee was formed to bring a concrete proposal back to the congregation at a special congregational meeting scheduled for the end of February. I was given permission to do initial interviews at a denominational conference I had planned to attend before that meeting. The committee met twice and put together a proposal, including a job description and budget. This proposal was mailed out to all church members a few weeks before the February meeting. The congregation met, discussed, and approved the proposal. We had two potential candidates out during the month of March. The search committee met with each candidate and presented a candidate on the first Sunday in April. The congregation unanimously accepted the recommendation of the search committee. The call was extended and accepted.

I feel that we set a world record for the establishment of a new full-time staff position in a church. There was history with youth ministry that preceded this, but the idea of a full-time youth pastor had not been presented to the congregation before the meeting in January. There is no question in my mind that this decision was made so easily because of the trust that had been developed within our system and the momentum that had been established in our ministries in large part because of this trust. The great thing, however, about having a radical commitment to congregational decision-making is that things move along more quickly and effectively than they otherwise would. Good ideas can be presented to congregations without months or even years of discussion in committees. Then, difficult and challenging decisions can be made quickly and collectively. This idea about hiring a youth pastor was clearly seen as good, but challenging. It pushed us to take a leap of faith and faithfulness.

5
Persuading Your People

I recently had a conversation with a pastor from a church I helped restructure. I helped their church downsize and centralize their church government within the context of a radical commitment to congregational decision-making. I called this pastor six months after they made these changes to ask how things were going. When this pastor reflected on their most recent church-council meetings, she said the amazing thing was that "everything we do seems meaningful." Under their previous board system, most of their meetings felt like a waste of time. Little seemed to get accomplished, and what did get accomplished did not seem to matter, even to those on these administrative boards.

PROMISES YOU CAN KEEP

To get your churches to try this new type of system, start by promising fewer meetings. Most churches and pastors are fed up with the number of administrative meetings they have to attend, particularly when meetings are not purposeful or significant. There is usually little resistance to the idea of eliminating committees and meetings—particularly when establishing a system of trust is your primary goal. Shrinking government and downsizing bureaucracies are often very appealing to congregations. Simplifying systems and eliminating unnecessary meetings are something for which most churches yearn. We simply need to say we can do it by restructuring.

Kennon Callahan writes,

> The purpose of the church is to involve people in God's mission in the world, to involve them in worship that is corporate and dynamic and in a group wherein they experience significant rela-

tionships of sharing and caring. The central driving purpose of the church is not to involve people in committee meeting after committee meeting. Indeed, it is highly possible for a member of a congregation to be significantly involved in the church's mission in the world, significantly involved in worship, and significantly involved in a major group of solid relationships and to invest very little time serving on committees.[1]

Church leaders within overgrown church systems tell me their nominating committees have to promise people that they will not have to attend all the meetings or participate in any of the activities just to get them to agree to take positions. Therefore, people fill these positions without any vested interest in their ministries just so congregations can be in compliance with their constitution and by-laws. Boards are dragged down, and people in these churches are left feeling frustrated and discouraged.

With too much structure, you also run the risk of getting people on your boards who want authority, not responsibility. When you simplify your system and one leader from the church council ends up focusing on an entire area within the life of the church, there will inevitably be both responsibility and authority associated with these positions. Leadership roles end up being more clearly defined, and people who tend to cause problems end up being very transparent to the congregation and its leaders. It eventually takes people who want the authority to control without the responsibility to minister out of leadership positions altogether.

In his book *Clergy Killers,* G. Lloyd Rediger, a church leader specializing in clergy leadership issues, points out how destructive individuals can become within churches, both for pastors and congregations. Rediger writes,

> We are not just talking about conflict anymore, we are talking about emotional and spiritual abuse of traumatic proportions. And we are discovering that such abuse is exhausting pastors and draining the energy and resources of congregations and denominational programs.[2]

Rediger continues, "And pastors must not allow themselves to slip into victim-thinking, in which they become pitiful shadows of a once noble profession. It will be up to pastors to break this degenerative pattern and move the church forward toward health."[3]

Rediger places a lot of blame on the individuals he calls "clergy killers." He effectively points out that there are sick people in our churches that leave the churches and clergy vulnerable to "attacks." My theory is that our best defense is a good offense. We need to protect our congregations from the "sick" people we are trying to serve by keeping our structures simple and by making sure these people do not end up in leadership positions. Interestingly, the demand of both responsibility and authority from these positions helps take care of this by itself. Sick people who want authority without responsibility have a hard time bearing their responsibilities, and they typically end up leaving their positions or not seeking them in the first place.

EFFECTIVELY USING TIME

In his book *The Once and Future Church*, Loren Mead, founder of the Alban Institute, talks about how the church needs to change to be prepared to do ministry in our changing world. Speaking about local congregations, Mead writes, "It is harder and harder to maintain the congregational structure and systems that have served so many generations so well."[4]

However, Mead continues, "In this climate, many respond by trying harder and harder to do the old thing better. They try to turn the clock back to the familiar dream of the Christendom Paradigm, working to resurrect an antiquarian institution."[5]

Churches need to find new ways to function in an age where time is valued almost as much as money. Most people today are not so emotionally sick that we need to be afraid of them, but most people are so busy that we do need to fear misusing their time and energy.

There was a day when the pace of life was more conducive to hosting large, bureaucratic, church governments. However, people no longer have the time for this and want their time to be used more effectively. Mead writes, "The need for imaginative, caring ministries that reach out to the community is greater than ever. But both laity and clergy face the new challenge unclear about their roles and unclear about how to move ahead."[6]

Streamlining our systems and downsizing our church governments can help. Encouraging people to participate in ministry rather than on administrative boards will, too. We can promise people their time and energy will be used in better ways.

BEING EFFECTIVELY LESS ORGANIZED

There are occasions when being less organized creates problems. However, these problems are miniscule in comparison with the problems that accompany overgrown church systems. Problems are responded to quickly and resolutions are sought assertively. Some things will fall through the cracks. However, they do so without disrupting our ministries. There is far less micromanaging in each particular area of ministry and many more people thinking about the big picture. Issues are responded to quickly because of this new level of agility.

The exciting thing about making these kinds of changes is that people begin to take more responsibility for their role as members of the church. They begin to realize that there is more to being a member than sitting in a pew or being on a board or committee. Members begin to realize that everyone in the church ought to have a personal ministry and that their ministry can combine both formal opportunities to minister, such as teaching Sunday school or serving communion, and informal opportunities to minister, such as visiting someone who is home-bound or tutoring a young person struggling with school.

One innovative way of thinking about each member's ministry is through the concept of a portfolio. A portfolio is typically a collection of an artist's work that reveals the wide range of his or her talents. With regard to ministry, each member can develop a portfolio filled with a wide range of activities within the church. Church members can be expected to be responsible for at least three or four things within the church. Each member's portfolio will be different and will not be confined to any one particular area. One person may teach Sunday school, sing in the choir, plant flowers on a seasonal basis, and visit an inmate in a local prison. Another person may volunteer in the church office, lead an adult Bible study, volunteer in the nursery, and at a soup kitchen once a month. Still, another may volunteer to do construction work around the church, to teach Sunday school, to work with Habitat for Humanity, and to serve as vice chair on the church council.

People are happiest when they are using their gifts and abilities creatively and enthusiastically. People want to be involved with the whole life of the church. They enjoy variety and would prefer not to feel confined by unnecessary structure within the church system. People enjoy the flexibility and freedom offered by a centralized church structure, and they enjoy being committed to the church out of a sense of freedom, not obligation.

An Experiment

You could propose these changes to your congregation as an experiment. Suggest a two-or three-year trial period. I know of one church that simply voted to suspend a certain section of their constitution for two years, which gave them the freedom to establish a smaller, more centralized church government immediately. People are often willing to try just about anything on a trial basis. If presented as a permanent, inflexible change, people may let their fears get the best of them. A "try and see" attitude will help your people commit to the process.

In *The Once and Future Church*, Mead tells a story about being asked to watch the Super Bowl at a friend's house. Mead writes, "We sat in his den, my wife and I, he and his wife. At the half time his four teenage children roared in with the Cokes and pretzels and six friends. We could no longer fit into the den. We had to move the TV to the living room, shift all the furniture around, and reorganize ourselves to see the second half. We had to change nearly everything to go on doing what we had already been doing and wanted to continue."[7]

If churches want to continue doing what they have been doing in ministry, they may have to shift things around structurally. Downsizing your structure and streamlining your systems could be compared to "rearranging your furniture," so that your church can more effectively do what Christ has always called you to do.

These changes provide an opportunity for our churches to start over structurally from square one. Churches can then add ministry teams if needed down the road. Starting with a small, centralized church government gives you a clean slate. Shrinking your church government feels like a new start for your congregation. And if you do end up forming additional ministry teams, these ministry teams will most likely end up being more action-oriented and less administrative in nature. It will help them to see that the ultimate goal is to help the church function better and to become more clearly focused upon mission and ministry.

Being open to the idea of additional structure in the future will also reassure those concerned about there not being enough structure that more can be added if necessary. A few years after downsizing to a single group of leaders, our church started to grow and so did our leadership demands. At this time, our church developed a second group of leaders called the Fellowship Council. The Fellowship Council oversees all things related to food, fun, and fellowship. What we discovered was that these fellowship items were typically the last things on our Church Council's agenda and were not receiving the full attention they deserved. We had a fellowship coordinator, but as we grew, so did the demands for leadership and organization at our special events.

The Fellowship Council effectively met these leadership needs within the life of our congregation. What was last on the Church Council's agenda is now first on the Fellowship Council's. Their focus is completely different, and there seems to be very few overlapping agenda items. The Fellowship Council is appreciated by the Church Council, and vice-versa. The Fellowship Council also understands that they are not responsible for overseeing the ministries of our church.

POINT TO TRUST

Building trust is a great focal point for leading your congregation into these changes. Leaders must demonstrate that trust is the goal and that you want the congregation to be a part of it. Convincing them that you are serious about this radical commitment to making decisions congregationally is essential. It is a key to the success of your proposal and to the implementation of these ideas. If they honestly believe that you will bring all major decisions before them, they will place their trust in you and allow this change to take place. You ultimately need to begin by entrusting your congregation with this decision about restructuring. They will need to take ownership of the new structure if it is going to work.

Present your case clearly. It is best to boldly lay out the facts in a straightforward and open manner. It is also essential that people be given an opportunity to express their thoughts and opinions. There are positives and negatives with every proposal. In this case, the positives far outweigh the negatives. If you put all the positives and negatives of this proposal out in the open, the scales will tip in the direction of making these changes. Nevertheless, you must go through the process of educating your congregation and allowing for open, honest discussion.

There will probably be a few people within your church who are dead set against these changes. You should not keep these individuals from speaking their minds, but neither should you let these individuals keep your congregation from voting on this matter. There will always be some people who do not like the decisions we make congregationally. However, mature Christians will be able to handle any decision made in an open and fair way. The worst possible scenario is educating people about developing a radical commitment to making decisions congregationally and then not allowing them to utilize it in relationship to this very significant decision. Do not let one or two people keep you from voting on something so significant. This will seal your fate in the past, and it will keep your congregation from reaching its full potential for Jesus Christ. It will feed the church monster and, in turn, the church monster will keep feeding on you.

Realistic Expectations

When I first came to Salem Covenant Church, I noticed the chair of our diaconate was very frustrated. On paper, the deacons were expected to do more than anyone else in the church. They were charged with the spiritual and pastoral care of our entire congregation. They were also encouraged to focus on evangelism, outreach, worship, member care, and more. The list of potential responsibilities was endless, and since it was impossible to do all that generally was expected, they fell into a pattern of doing only that that was specifically required. Once a month, they set up and served communion. Since the deacons were always left feeling they could be doing more, they were not even able to enjoy what they were able to accomplish.

UNCLEAR AND UNFAIR EXPECTATIONS

My immediate response was to lower the unrealistic expectations so the chairperson and the diaconate could feel good about what they were doing. Evangelism, outreach, worship, and member care are the responsibilities of the whole church, not just one particular group. These particular ministries should grow out of the people's interests and spiritual gifts, not out of being elected to a particular board.

Eventually, we allowed the board of deacons to disintegrate with all the other boards in the church, and I asked the person representing diaconate concerns on the Church Council simply to set up and serve communion each month. I encouraged her to see every member in our church as a deacon and said that she could use any of them to help serve communion. I wanted her and those serving communion to feel good about what they were doing.

In his book *Transforming Congregations for the Future*, Loren Mead states, "Volunteers within a congregation need to get some clarity about what is expected of them and what resources they can count on to do their jobs. Otherwise they are pushed into the childish position of having to fantasize what is expected against the backdrop that one can never do enough. It is no wonder that volunteers burn out and grow resentful of how they have been treated."[1]

People in leadership positions not only need to know how much authority they have, but also how much responsibility. A downsized church government is far more realistic about how much can be expected of each leader and how much needs to be expected of other volunteers who will be called on to help. There are limits to what we can expect of our leaders, and if others do not volunteer to help, blame should not fall on the leaders, but rather upon the lack of commitment revealed within our congregations as a whole.

Even though chairpersons within board systems are supposed to have active boards working with them, many of these chairpersons end up bearing the entire burden of responsibility. If things are not getting done within a particular area, they are the ones who receive the criticism. These individuals then either get depressed because they feel that they are failing, or they get angry because they feel the other board members are failing. The problem is the endless number of expectations associated with each board and the inactivity of board members who fear getting in over their heads.

People should feel good about what they do for the church, and they should be able to choose different levels of participation. If people want to try dipping their toes in the waters of responsibility, they should be able to do this without feeling as though someone else is going to come up out of the water and pull them into the deep end. This essentially is what happens when individuals are asked to be on boards without much being expected of them, and then having other people get upset and angry with them when they are not doing enough. Most church boards are filled with expectations and void of the gratitude and appreciation volunteers deserve. By simplifying your system through downsizing and centralizing, you leave more room for gratitude and appreciation and less room for unrealistic expectations.

TRAPPED IN LEADERSHIP

Another common problem in local churches occurs when individuals feel trapped in leadership positions despite conflicting demands in their personal lives. Key leaders often feel obligated to stay in their positions because the church is already having a difficult time filling positions. When things get to be too much in their personal lives, the people in these positions have no place to turn. In many instances, individuals either blow up, melt down, leave the church, or become completely inactive because they could not find another way out.

It is essential to make clear to all people in leadership positions that, if the responsibility is too overwhelming, they have the right and even the responsibility to resign from their positions. The good news is that with a smaller, more manageable group of leaders, there is always a sense that there are other people out there who can fill positions if someone cannot handle the responsibilities at any particular point in time. Thus, if something is going on in someone's personal life or career that makes it impossible for this person to stay in their position, there is no reason why they cannot ask to be replaced. At Salem Covenant Church, we have had several people resign from their positions on the Church Council and simultaneously stay very active within the church on other levels.

AUTHORITY AND RESPONSIBILITY

Smaller church governments make it impossible for power-hungry people to have authority without responsibility. If nominating committees, desperate to fill vacancies within their overgrown church governments, promise minimal responsibility while freely giving authority to anyone willing to attend an occasional committee meeting, none of us should be surprised by the amount of conflict and anxiety embedded in our church systems. Giving individuals authority without responsibility empowers them to become the "well-intentioned dragons" described by Marshall Shelly or the "clergy killers" described by G. Lloyd Rediger. Authority without responsibility is a formula for disaster. It is one reason why it can be so difficult to rid ourselves of the church monster.

Having responsibility associated with leadership positions is essential. In part, this is why smaller church structures are more effective and less volatile. With smaller, centralized church structures, the lines are clearer between those who are participating in our ministries and those who are the leaders organizing the ministries. Troublemakers become very apparent, and serious problems become isolated and manageable. Space is offered for all people to participate in the worship and ministries of a church. However, authority is limited to those who are able to handle it and who are willing to bear the responsibility that goes with it.

A simplified church system encourages leaders to be leaders and allows the people who tend to create problems to focus upon their own problems and to receive the kind of help and care they should be able to receive from other church members and the church in general.

Frank Tillapaugh writes, "If the church is going to concentrate on front-line ministries it must select people it can trust to do the rear-echelon management and give them the authority to do it."[2]

AVOIDING TRIANGULAR RELATIONSHIPS

One of the keys to keeping personal conflict from getting out of control in your church is avoiding and discouraging triangular relationships. Edwin Friedman, a rabbi and family therapist who first applied family theory to clergy and congregations, writes, "An emotional triangle is formed by any three persons or issues." Friedman continues, "A person may be said to be 'triangled' if he or she gets caught in the middle as the focus of such an unresolved issue."[3] It is important to stay out of the middle of unresolved conflict that other people experience. And I try to keep people out of the middle of any unresolved conflict I may be experiencing with someone else in the congregation. Friedman states, "We can only change a relationship to which we belong. Therefore, the way to bring change to the relationship of two others (and no one said it is easy) is to try to maintain a well-defined relationship with each and to avoid the responsibility for their relationship with one another."[4]

It is hard in overgrown, complicated church structures to avoid getting caught in the middle of things. Pastors and lay leaders continually find themselves being triangled among boards, committees, and other individuals. They even find themselves being triangled in relationship to issues that have little, if any, significance to them personally. Pastors often find that they end up having to continually fight off being caught in the middle of issues that do not matter to them. This is when ministry begins to lose its focus and meaning for them. It is why many clergypersons become discouraged and distracted within their ministries.

The good news is that the vast majority of people in our church systems seek to avoid getting in the middle of church conflict and administration. They want some responsibility for our church ministries, but they do not want to be involved in the day-to-day decision-making. This is why most people would rather participate in ministries than be on boards. They prefer not to be in the middle of things, because they know how challenging that can be. Our goal as church leaders should be to accommodate these people and present opportunities for them to be actively involved with our ministries without having any obligation to be involved with making decisions. The ministry is what matters most, not the management of these ministries. Their management matters only insofar as it affects the quality of our ministries.

VARIETY AND COMMITMENT

Smaller church governments have to rely on a wide range of volunteers. Church leaders cannot just see a problem and say "that is the trustee's responsibility" or "that is the responsibility of the deacons." They have to think about which individuals they could approach to help them out with certain projects or problems. They have to think about real people with real names. Individuals must be approached persuasively, not coercively. Church leaders must motivate and mobilize a variety of people to do a variety of tasks, or things will not get done. Under such circumstances, people are not forced to do things because they are a part of a board; rather, they are asked to do things because they are a part of a church.

The exciting thing is that individuals are also being encouraged to consider being involved with a broader range of church activities and ministries. There are many highly committed, creative, and talented members of Salem Covenant Church who shift around or adjust their responsibilities each year, based on where they feel led to utilize their gifts. I have learned to be flexible with these people because I know that they will give more of themselves if they are excited about what they are doing. I have even gotten to a place within my leadership where I am curious to see what exciting new things these individuals might do next to strengthen our ministries.

William Easum writes about churches that rely on spiritual gifts rather than church boards to determine who will do what within the life of a church's ministries. Easum writes, "Laity develop long-term expertise in a particular area which they can use to train others who have their same gift, but no expertise."[5]

In a system like this, everyone is encouraged to have a ministry or several ministries. Not everyone is asked to be in a leadership position, but all are asked to be involved with ministry and to discover not just where they can contribute, but also where God might be calling them to be involved.

Dramatic Change

I once saw a television documentary about a place in China where the primary industry was bamboo scaffolding. Scaffolding is a temporary structure used by workers to support them while they are building, painting, or doing other work in high places. Most scaffolding in the United States is made out of steel. Thus, it was strange to see pictures of scaffolding made out of bamboo. The broadcaster asked the owner of this business why they did not use steel. The owner indicated that bamboo scaffolding withstands strong storms better than steel. He said that at one point in time, there were two buildings next to each other—one had bamboo scaffolding and the other steel. When a typhoon hit, the bamboo scaffolding remained intact, while the steel scaffolding fell to the ground. When the reporter asked why, he explained that steel scaffolding is too rigid, whereas the bamboo scaffolding has enough flexibility to withstand storms.

STRUCTURE AND FLEXIBILITY

Churches need flexibility within their structures to face the storms in which they find themselves. Developing smaller, more centralized church governments with a radical commitment to making decision congregationally provides the needed structure and flexibility. These systems will lift our churches up with the right amount of structure to do the work that Jesus Christ has called us to do. However, they will also provide enough flexibility for our churches to be able to weather the storms of church conflict and societal change.

William Easum writes, "We are the first generation of immigrant North Americans to live in a society that no longer appreciates the presence of Christianity."[1]

There is a huge paradigm shift taking place in our society, and it presents both big challenges and huge opportunities for our churches. In his book *Transforming Congregations for the Future*, Loren Mead writes about the storm most churches find themselves in today. Mead writes,

> I deeply believe that the storm we are in presents the greatest opportunity the churches and religious leaders have ever had. Bar none. I also believe it is a deeper challenge and threat than religious leaders have faced in many centuries. We are in serious trouble that we will not get out of soon or easily. When we get clear of this storm, our religious institutions may bear little resemblance to those which we grew up in.[2]

One element of our churches that will need to change if we are to survive all this is the way they function. Churches cannot continue wasting the time and energy of people. More effective, efficient structures are a necessity for weathering this storm and becoming the mission outposts needed in a culture that no longer appreciates the church in the way it did in the past. Things must begin to change now!

Cold Turkey Change

It is best for churches to dramatically change their church systems all at once. Churches should downsize and centralize their church governments and develop a radical commitment to congregational decision-making simultaneously. I am suggesting a "cold turkey" approach, which means immediately and all at once. What took years of gradual process to develop at Salem Covenant Church is something you can do through a series of informational and action-oriented meetings.

Why not give the members of your congregation the opportunity to read this book or to hear a summary of this book before you have your meetings? Then have congregational gatherings to discuss the possibilities for this type of dramatic structural change. At the final congregational meeting, your church could make concrete decisions that would help to downsize and centralize your church government.

One church I advised did this in three meetings. I met with their executive board; then with all their boards and any interested church members; they then had a congregational meeting and made the decision to give this new structure a try. Structural changes can happen this quickly, but it will take time for churches to adjust to a new way of doing things and to fine-tune the way members function together. The good news is that, in a matter of a few meetings, it is possible for churches to establish a new structure that will give them the foundation on which they can build an entirely new future.

The circumstances were such at Salem Covenant Church that this new structure evolved through a series of events and decisions. The church was discouraged and experiencing so much conflict that they were willing to try anything. Slowly but surely, we figured out what needed to be done and implemented these changes incrementally. It would have been much easier to have a plan approved before we got started, but such a plan did not exist, so we improvised and developed it as we went along. Developing a radical commitment to making decisions congregationally was really the key that helped us to open the door to these new realities for our church. It made all the other structural changes possible.

The temptation is to go only part way and to try a gradual approach, like shrinking but not centralizing your church government. This will not resolve the real issues. It does not eliminate the possibility for power struggles to develop between groups of leaders, and it keeps the church from turning to the congregation with the difficult questions. It is best for churches to go all the way and downsize and centralize their church governments first and, then, if needed, add structure in the future.

In his book *Moving Off the Map*, Thomas Bandy writes,

> Systemic change is both revolutionary and evolutionary. It is revolutionary in that it demands an entirely new way of thinking and behaving that dramatically contrasts with past thinking and behavior. It is evolutionary in that change in one subsystem of congregational life leads to another subsystem and then to another subsystem and so on and on."[3]

Churches can make revolutionary changes through downsizing and centralizing. Nevertheless, there will be all sorts of evolutionary change that will follow and emerge from this structural revolution. This is just the first step in our battle with the church monster, but once this step is taken, the monster will begin to weaken and, eventually, will fall.

STARTING OVER AGAIN

There has been a strong emphasis on church planting within my denomination over the past several years. Usually a mission-minded pastor is called into a new area and develops a new church with a core group of interested, mission-minded laypeople. These new congregations may meet in various homes to start and then, possibly, a meeting hall or auditorium, before they actually buy land and erect a building. Before anything is built, however, they have to establish a church structure. I have discovered that our denominational leaders most often recommend these church plants start with small, centralized church governments.

Restructuring can help older established congregations feel young again, but making these changes "cold turkey" requires a leap of faith and courage on the part of congregations and their pastors. Your church won't change entirely, but the way you make decisions will. This will help your church to experience new life and vitality in other areas of your ministries as well. There will be a spin-off affect from this change, producing all kinds of other change that can lead into an entirely new beginning for a congregation. God not only wants us to survive the storms we experience, God wants us to thrive while we experience sunny days and seasons of growth as well.

TOOLS FOR CHANGE

A decision to dramatically change your church structure will require your church to go through a period of adjustment. Inevitably, there will be a feeling of instability for a time, stemming from the newfound flexibility of a smaller church government, and yet there will be an alternative type of newfound stability that will come with a radical commitment to congregational decision-making. It will indeed take time for all of this to settle down and for your church to adjust to these new realities.

In working with other congregations to implement these changes, I have found that leaders want to know how new leaders will be developed and how responsibilities will be transferred. When these fears and questions arise, I typically end up sharing information about church management tools that helped Salem Covenant Church to maintain administrative stability. Some of the key tools to which I am referring are job descriptions, time and talent pledge cards, term limits, a vice chair position, and an annual leadership orientation meeting.

Detailed job descriptions enable individual leaders to be aware of their specific responsibilities. For example, the head trustee needs to know when to order fuel for heating the church and when to form a new contract with the company or individual that mows your church lawns. These kinds of details can easily be included in a job description and information on how to do these things can be included as well. The same would apply to your Christian-education coordinator, who would need to know when to order curriculum and when to make sure teachers are being recruited before classes begin.

Church Council members are not responsible for doing everything in each of their areas of concern. They are, however, responsible for delegating and making sure tasks are being completed. At first glance, the responsibilities of our Christian-education coordinator might seem unmanageable and overwhelming, but, in reality, our Sunday-school superintendent in many ways has more responsibility for the running of our Sunday-school programs than does the coordinator. We also have one person who coordinates our church nursery, another our Vacation Bible School, another our camp scholarship fundraising, and so on. The pastor oversees adult Christian education, and so the Christian-education coordinator ends up being in charge of attending Church Council meetings, facilitating communication, and supporting our ministries in whatever ways she or he feels called.

Another tool that may help during a system changeover is the "time-and-talent-pledge card." When your church does its annual stewardship campaign, include a pledge card that allows people to indicate where they might be interested in serving your church. For example, if people indicate they are interested in serving as a greeter, usher, or lay reader, their names can be placed on a list given to the church secretary who schedules all such volunteers. Or if the box is checked next to the words "Sunday School Teacher," that person's name can be given to the Christian-education coordinator in charge of recruiting teachers in cooperation with our Sunday-school superintendent.

Another tool to help people feel good about making these changes is term limits. Most churches already have term limits on their leadership positions. However, within small, centralized church governments, people can actually get well-needed breaks from being in these primary, leadership positions. When church structure is overgrown, church leaders often end up changing positions in the system, but they rarely, if ever, get a break from leadership, unless they resign altogether or leave and go elsewhere. In a small, centralized church government, leadership roles are a big responsibility, but they are not permanent, and people simply takes turns bearing the brunt of the leadership responsibilities.

One vital position on the Church Council that is often overlooked is the vice chair position. It is essential to have someone to run meetings in the absence of the church chair, but it is also significant in that the vice chairperson can be designated as the head of the stewardship committee. At Salem Covenant Church, our stewardship and vision committee facilitates our annual faith-pledge drive and educates the congregation on the benefits of whole-life stewardship. The stewardship and vision committee does not set the vision for our church but, rather, seeks to communicate the vision established by the pastor, other church leaders, and our congregation.

A final tool worth mentioning is our leadership orientation meeting. This is always the first meeting we host each year at Salem Covenant Church. It is critical at this meeting to teach new church leaders about the benefits of making decisions congregationally. It is here where I explain why we are committed to bringing all the significant decisions before the congregation. We talk about where the authority of the Church Council comes from, where the pastor's authority comes from, and from where their authority as individual leaders will come. We talk about the limits of our authority as individuals and a group. We ultimately acknowledge that the congregation is the highest authority, followed by the Church Council, and then the pastor and other church leaders.

A Clearer Focus

Each one of these tools helps us to function more effectively within a system of a downsized and centralized church government. Other administrative tools may emerge that you will find even more helpful. The point here is there are ways to meet your church's administrative needs without building up unnecessary layers of bureaucracy. Churches can function well with a simple system of leadership and a flexible approach to ministry. You may not cross every "t" or dot every "i," but you will bring glory to God through a clearer focus upon mission and ministry.

Speaking about the early church, William Easum writes,

> Leadership in the early communities was based on faithful service to Christ. Leadership was defined as servanthood. Titles were avoided. Authority was based on how they lived rather than how much they knew. Trust and respect were earned through service to others. Emphasis was placed on an individual's spiritual gifts. Since no formal church structure existed, the early church encouraged people to discover their God-given gifts rather than fit into a particular need of the church.[4]

I am convinced the future church must have less structure than it currently does, but also that it will need some structure to flourish. The key will be discerning how much structure will be enough without falling into the trap of having too much. The goal, once again, should be less-organized churches, not disorganized religion. The aim is to make life miserable for the monster and conducive to a focus on mission and ministry.

Part 2

MOVING FORWARD

Courageous Congregations

During my first few weeks of ministry at Salem Covenant Church, I invited the members of the church to participate in "focus groups." Members of the church were asked to sign up in small groups to come and talk with me about what they wanted to see happen in the life of our church. Listening to what people had to say helped me realize that they wanted to grow, both in terms of size and togetherness. This understanding, in turn, helped us to establish a clear vision for our future. We knew where we wanted to go. The question was, how were we going to get there?

STARTING WITH SMALL STEPS

The first few years of pursuing our goals moved slowly but surely. We focused on a few small projects, like ordering a new music book to supplement our hymnal. We purchased puppets to begin a puppet ministry, and we put up high-quality basketball hoops in our parking lot for the community to use. We achieved the latter two goals through fundraisers called "Hoops for Jesus" and "Puppets for Kids." Success with these small projects brought some much-needed momentum to our ministries.

We also made several changes to become a more visitor-friendly church. We added "Visitor Parking" signs in our church parking lot and added signs in our church building indicating where the bathrooms, the offices, the Sunday-school rooms, and the fellowship areas were located. In the worship service itself, I added a special welcome to guests and visitors after the general welcome to everyone at the beginning of our worship service. And, during our offering, I also indicate that guests and visitors are not expected to offer anything financially by saying, "We are simply glad you are here." Then I add,

"But if you are a member or are committed to the ministries of our church, please respond to God's grace and love by bringing your tithes and offerings." We also include a statement at the bottom of our bulletin each Sunday that again welcomes guests and visitors and indicates that one of our church's goals is to "create an environment where all people feel loved and accepted by each other so we can, in turn, gain a clearer understanding of ourselves and our God."

Making changes like these and completing a few small, but significant, projects helped our congregation to build its confidence and to begin expecting guests and visitors to come. We not only began expecting visitors, but we also started to see them return on following Sundays. Becoming more visitor-friendly helped our entire congregation become more aware of how important a warm welcome is, and having some momentum from the small projects we were doing helped us to feel better about what we were doing in general.

Celebrating small accomplishments makes it possible for simple projects to turn into big endeavors. Small changes have tremendous potential to lead congregations toward major change and transformation. Thomas Bandy writes, "The ability to discern hope is more than optimism that good will triumph in the end. It is the perceptiveness that identifies potential and teases it out of the fabric of life. It is the ability to shift back and forth from the macro to the micro and to see the smallest detail as a fulcrum that can shift the course of history."[1]

The recognition that something small may lead to something big may not seem overly insightful. However, many pastors get into trouble when they go into congregations and seek to make huge changes within their first few weeks or months of ministry. Many pastors mistakenly believe that if they can get major changes through in the first few months, their churches will be destined for a much brighter future. However, more often than not, these changes backfire, freeze up the system, and leave the pastor and any cooperating lay leaders vulnerable and discouraged. Broken trust is very difficult to mend.

Starting with small changes that the congregation can readily agree to leaves room for momentum to emerge and for serious change or transformation to take place at a later date in the midst of a more established relationship between the congregation and its pastor.

Trying to push congregations into taking steps they are not prepared to take runs a high risk of failure. If too much change is introduced too soon, congregations become paralyzed by their fear of change. This is why encouraging your congregation to take a few small steps to start can help to establish initial motion in your system. As a congregation begins to feel good about what it is accomplishing, individuals begin to feel enthusiastic about being a part of a church where things are happening. Therefore, wise leaders begin by introducing change incrementally and progressively.

Thomas Bandy writes,

> Church transformation can begin at any point, and at any place, in the system of congregational life. One begins where it is easiest to begin. That is, begin where permission is easiest to obtain. Energy wasted in combat trying to force change against strong resistance lowers moral, alienates leadership, and makes all subsequent change more difficult. Systemic change moves from celebration to celebration, rather than from victory to victory. The celebration of one successful experiment motivates the congregation to take greater subsequent risks."[2]

The small projects that have helped our church build its confidence and develop momentum did indeed lead us to take "greater subsequent risks." And having a radical commitment to making decisions congregationally helped to ensure that this was perceived as a movement from "celebration to celebration," rather than "victory to victory." If we see the changes we make in our churches as victories, then there are winners and losers within our congregations. If we are able to celebrate accomplishments together, then everyone wins, and we can all feel good about what we are doing.

THE PERFECTION MYTH

Many churches become paralyzed by "the perfection myth." This is the myth that says that churches are supposed to be perfect and that there is no room for weakness or brokenness. There is weakness and brokenness in all of our churches. Nevertheless, many churches become paralyzed and discouraged by their weaknesses. They compare themselves to other churches and cannot get their minds off what other churches are doing. These churches become paranoid by their imperfections and stop believing that anyone would actually choose to join their church.

Kennon Callahan argues that when churches begin to examine their ministries and plan for the future, they should begin by focusing upon their strengths, not their weaknesses. In a discussion about strategic, long-range planning, Callahan writes, "The first strategic decision in successful long-range planning is to help a congregation to find and claim its present central strengths. . . . Substantial power is generated as a congregation discovers and claims its strengths."[3]

Only after identifying and coming up with a plan to expand these strengths does Callahan suggest making decisions with regard to "which new foundational strengths to add that are commensurate with and build on those already in place."[4]

I remember telling the people at Salem Covenant Church to stop comparing themselves to other churches. This always brought our attention to the things we were not doing well. Churches too focused on perfection and competition only see what they are doing wrong. They rarely, if ever, see what they are doing right. Squashing the perfection myth allows churches to focus on their strengths rather than weaknesses. As Salem became stronger, we were able to more effectively address our weaknesses over time. Callahan writes, "In the coming years, we need more churches that are interested in success and fewer churches that are preoccupied with their own problems."[5]

CONGREGATIONAL COURAGE

Another very exciting discovery we have made at Salem Covenant Church with regard to making decisions together is that congregations generally are more courageous than committees or boards, particularly when trust has been developed between the congregation and its leaders. Congregations are more courageous because committees and boards are constantly trying to figure out what their congregations will think about specific issues, and they tend to be cautious if they think even a few members of their congregation might not like something. Making your decisions congregationally eliminates this kind of guesswork and anxiety and keeps a few people from putting the brakes on potentially great ideas.

Because congregations are typically more courageous than committees, the potential for courage within our congregations is much larger than we often think. Leaders need to focus on developing congregational courage. Starting with small, consensus-building decisions is one way to begin building courage. Focusing on improvements rather than perfection is another, as is seeking to establish trust within your system.

Restructuring will help to make your congregation become more courageous than you ever imagined it could be, but this will take time and patience. You can quickly change the structure of your system, but transforming the attitude and approach of your congregation is a process, not an event. The important thing is that you are moving forward, and your congregation is being prepared for this type of transformation.

Congregations also need courageous pastors and leaders who are willing to take risks that will help lead the membership of their churches to grow spiritually. I am not talking about taking risks with regard to how we make decisions but, rather, about taking risks with regard to the kind of decisions we ask our congregations to make. I am talking about asking people to participate in ministry more radically and about establishing a vision and a ministry agenda that will push our churches to serve others more fully. Challenging your congregation with an aggressive ministry agenda is a risk worth taking.

Building up the courage and the confidence of your congregations will help you become more focused on mission and ministry. Your church will turn its focus off of its problems and on to its potential. Churches will be freed up to become the churches God wants them to be. God does not want our churches to become frozen or paralyzed by our fears and insecurities. God wants us to become more confident and courageous with regard to everything we do. Having confidence and courage in our congregations can inspire a great deal of change and enthusiasm. It moves our focus from ourselves to God and from decision-making to discipleship.

I will never forget the sermon preached at the ordination service of a friend of mine. A very unimposing, older, ordained woman came to the pulpit to speak. She spoke saying that no matter how developed or sophisticated our ministries become, we will never catch up with Jesus. Jesus will always be out ahead of us. We fool ourselves when we think we can catch up with him. She pointed out that, as Christians, we are, by nature, followers and that even when we are called into leadership positions, we should not forget about who we are and what we have been called to do. We need to get the focus off of ourselves and on to Christ.

9
Unstoppable Momentum

A few years ago, I watched a children's television show called *Science Court* with my kids in which they talked about momentum. Momentum is defined as mass combined with velocity. To illustrate the importance of mass with regard to momentum, they showed a small boat made of sticks going down a river at two miles an hour. Anyone could stick out a finger and keep this boat from moving forward. They then showed a large steel barge moving two miles per hour down the same river. It was quite obvious no one person could ever stop this barge from moving forward, even though they were moving at the same speed. Greater mass makes for greater momentum.

Anything that combines a significant amount of mass with a significant amount of motion becomes virtually unstoppable. Making decisions congregationally has helped our church combine mass with movement. Most of the people at Salem Covenant Church feel a part of the decisions we make and the directions we take. This makes it very difficult for cynics and skeptics to restrict or limit the momentum our church has already established. Max De Pree, leadership expert and former CEO of Herman Miller, Inc., writes in his book *Leadership Is an Art*, "Leaders are obligated to provide and maintain momentum."[1]

CHANGE AND STABILITY

I once heard George Parsons of the Alban Institute speak about congregational change. He suggested that churches have to keep a balance between change and stability in order to create momentum. He drew a picture with two overlapping circles, and, in one circle, he wrote the word "change" and in the other, "stability." He suggested the area where the circles overlapped is where you want to be. Too much change or too much stability will limit momentum. Churches need just the right amount of both to really get things moving.[2]

Too many churches today fool themselves into thinking that there must be simple solutions to all of their major problems. There are no quick fixes. There are no gimmicks that will turn your church into a growing, thriving congregation. Changing your worship style or introducing a new program may impact your congregation dramatically, but unless these changes are embraced by your congregation and contribute to a general movement within your church, they will not have the sustained impact you desire.

Referring to a study conducted by Daniel V. Biles of the Alban Institute, William Easum writes,

> In short, the critical difference between healthy, growing congregations and other churches is not some secret formula for success. Their distinguishing feature is that they do the common, mundane, boring tasks of ministry uncommonly well. They do so regardless of their size, socioeconomic makeup, location, or environmental changes.[3]

Forcing major changes on your congregation without consent and cooperation will only lead to more conflict and struggle, even if these new initiatives make sense. Changes made with your people behind them will create an opportunity for movement and mass to exist simultaneously.

CONGREGATIONAL CHANGE

If church leaders isolate themselves from their congregations and try to make all the big decisions by themselves, they run the risk of alienating their congregations and keeping their vision from inspiring the momentum needed to keep churches moving forward. When an individual leader or a few people push their agenda through a church system without taking the time to develop congregational support, it not only leaves them mistrusted, but also leaves their ideas vulnerable because the movement is not backed up by the mass that is required to keep ideas and initiatives moving forward.

Making decisions congregationally helps to ensure a sense of ownership and belonging in the life of the congregation. It frees people up to be able to think about their actions in the church as a form of stewardship of all that God has entrusted to them. It helps people see themselves as members of the church and see membership in the church as something meaningful. It makes the management of ministry much easier and eliminates much of the friction that limits congregational momentum.

MAKING MAJOR DECISIONS

Most local churches have relatively few major decisions to make in any given year. I recently led a seminar at a conference for pastors and laypeople and asked those participating to count how many major decisions their churches have made over the past two or three years. None of them needed more than one hand. Why is it, then, that we spend so much time and energy on making decisions?

Many churches appear frozen in time because they do not know how to make major decisions. Having a trustworthy mechanism in place for making decisions together in a fair and open way can help churches implement change at a manageable and encouraging pace. A substantial commitment to referring difficult questions to congregations allows churches to make major changes when they need to be made.

Rest assured that your congregation will let you know when you are trying to introduce too much change at once. That said, most churches do not experience enough change because they fear too much change. If your congregation does not have a way to put the brakes on midstream, they may not even allow you to enter the water. But if your congregation does not allow some change, then the church monster we are trying to defeat will continue to have free reign in our congregations. An appropriate amount of change will make the monster's existence in your church less comfortable, if not intolerable.

EMBRACING GOOD IDEAS

Frank Tillapaugh writes about a general understanding they have at his church that helps them keep their administrative structure from becoming too complicated and enables them to respond quickly to ministry opportunities that arise. He writes, "We have an understanding in our ministry: If we become aware of a gospel need and have the resources to meet that need, the answer is yes."[4]

Most of the major decisions we make in our churches related to the mission of the church are positive in nature and rarely controversial—apart from the amount of time and money that will be required. Having less structure enables us to respond more quickly to ministry opportunities.

Many of our good ideas do not need congregational approval, because they are not controversial. For example, people may not like the topic of a small-group study, a retreat, or a workshop, but they do not have to participate if they are not interested. Most programs do not need preapproval. They simply need to be publicized, and people need to be encouraged to participate. The congregation does not need to make all ministry-related decisions but, rather, they need to help make decisions that are potentially controversial or anxiety-producing, whether they are ministry-related or not. Making all potentially controversial decisions in this way minimizes the potential for conflict. It also frees up your church to respond quickly to the ministry needs and opportunities that present themselves.

In his book, *The Purpose Driven Church*, Rick Warren writes, "Most people think of 'vision' as the ability to see the future. But in today's rapidly changing world, vision is also the ability to accurately assess current changes and to take advantage of them. Vision is being alert to opportunities."[5]

Seizing ministry opportunities is ultimately what will help us develop momentum in our ministries. However, if we try to do this without developing congregational support, momentum will not be possible. Good ideas can flourish in our congregations, but the people in our churches need to be asked to embrace these good ideas before they are forced on them. Congregations are capable of courage. Bad structure keeps church people from looking forward because they are so preoccupied with the poor way decisions have been made in the past.

FLEXIBILITY AND EXPERIMENTATION

When there is a radical commitment to having decisions made congregationally, churches seem to realize that no change is permanent and, thus, they tend to be more experimental and willing to take risks. If ideas are presented appropriately, at the right time within the life of a congregation, the church is typically willing to try new things. When churches feel that their leaders make significant decisions without them, they tend to react strongly against new ideas, whether they agree with them or not. When they are allowed to be a part of the discernment process, not only are they more willing to experiment, but they also seem to enjoy the experimentation taking place.

Thomas Bandy writes, "Initiative means that congregational participants take risks and church programming encourages experimentation."[6]

Developing an experimental atmosphere in your church not only encourages your church to try new things, it also allows you to be more flexible with regard to changing things back to the way they were if new initiatives fail. Salem Covenant Church has voted yes to some pretty ill-conceived ideas that I have suggested over the years simply because I felt that they were worth a try. Once it became obvious how ill conceived these ideas were, we promptly changed things back. This flexibility and willingness to experiment has helped our church respond more quickly in crises and when new ministry opportunities present themselves.

When you trust your congregation with the major decisions of your church, trust develops and so does openness to an appropriate amount of change and challenge. If change and challenge are introduced slowly in an environment of stability, momentum will develop. Churches will change if they feel they have the power to put on the brakes when things begin to change too quickly. It takes time and patience to develop momentum, life, and vitality in your church, but it can happen. No one decision or gimmick will transform your church, but when significant decisions are made consistently and collectively, transformation and renewal become likely possibilities.

PRIORITIZING MINISTRY

Tillapaugh refers to what he calls a "ministry first approach." He writes,

> The structure-first approach is one in which the structure is set and whatever ministry it spits out, the church does. That's much different from a ministry-first approach. This approach says that if we have the people who want to perform a certain ministry, we will build a structure around them.[7]

If a member at Salem Covenant Church wants to implement a ministry and there is nothing costly or contentious about their plan, we give them permission to begin. One example of this is our "Bread for Visitors" program. One woman was inspired to develop a ministry around bringing a homemade loaf of bread to first-time visitors. She was willing to check our attendance registries each week, to deliver the bread, and to ask other church members to make the bread. The church council gave her permission to begin and celebrated this new ministry at our next congregational meeting.

With regard to the future of the church, Thomas Bandy writes,

> The future of the church in the twenty-first century will not be determined by planning. It will be determined by leadership development. These leaders may be clergy or laity, and they will probably not care about the designation. They will be risk-takers and adventurers. They will always be wondering what opportunity lies over the next cultural hill. They will be explorers of the unknown. They will be you.[8]

At Salem Covenant Church, our initial challenge had to do with getting people to a place where they were comfortable being called leaders. Leadership is the ability and the willingness to bear the necessary responsibility and authority to make things happen. Overgrown church systems stifle leadership. If momentum is our goal, then space must be created for leadership. It is time to clear the way for leadership, momentum, and ministry to occur. It is time for churches to establish themselves as flexible and experimental. It is time for us to become less organized but more effective. It is time for new life and new beginnings. It is time to destroy the church monster and to refocus our attention on mission and ministry.

Meaningful Meetings

One of the most shocking realities Salem Covenant Church faced early in my ministry was the sharp contrast between the way we behaved in worship on Sunday mornings and the way we behaved in our quarterly congregational meetings. Our meetings were filled with chaos and confusion. The individuals with the loudest voices would win the discussions. Voting on motions rarely took place. The loudest voices simply led us into a half-baked form of consensus decision-making. Then I began trying to use my voice in an attempt to win these discussions, which only added to this sick system of chaotic congregational meetings. Members felt frustrated and felt that our meetings were not being run fairly or appropriately. They were right. This was the place where the church monster was most visible in the life of our congregation.

AS LITTLE AS POSSIBLE

In his book *Cannon's Concise Guide to Rules of Order*, Hugh Cannon, a professional parliamentarian, writes about his focus, saying, "The fundamental message of this book is that the rules of parliamentary procedure are simple and should be used as little as possible."[1]

I have come to realize how helpful *Robert's Rules of Order* are in this battle with the church monster, if used as much as necessary but as little as possible. I used to be repulsed by *Robert's Rules* because they seemed complex and some people try to use them as much as they can.

Cannon reveals how certain people can ruin the *Rules of Order* for everyone else in a group. He writes, "One of the worst mistakes a member can make is to challenge the Chair simply because a rule is not being followed with technical precision, that is, when the error does not in fact affect the substance or the fairness of the business at hand. This mistake is most often made by a member who is well schooled in parliamentary procedure and wishes to demonstrate this skill to the assembly."[2] Behavior like this in meetings has lead many people to feel that these rules of order are complicated and confusing.

USEFUL TOOLS

When used for the right reasons and with an appropriate amount of restraint, these rules of order can help you establish fair and effective meetings. And fair and effective meetings will help you to eventually defeat the church monster. To this end, there are a few key facts and a few wonderful tools that can help. First and foremost is that motions must be made before discussion begins. Discussing matters before a motion is presented often leads to confusion. A motion should be presented, debated, and amended when necessary. Then, most importantly, there needs to be a vote.

To avoid confusion, it is also helpful if substantive motions are written out ahead of time and delivered to members of the congregation before the meeting. To give background to a main motion, you can present the motion in the context of a resolution. "Whereas" statements preceding the main motion are quite effective for this purpose.[3]

If you are proposing new carpet in your sanctuary, for example, you might state: "Whereas, our sanctuary carpet is green and orange, and whereas it is no longer the 1970s; we move that we replace this green and orange carpet with red carpet." Someone may want to amend the main motion to make it blue, but the resolution will help people to know where the main motion is coming from and will provide some common ground for the discussion to follow. If an amendment is presented, it is discussed and voted on separately from the main motion. Once an amendment is voted on, the main motion can be discussed as amended, and voting can take place. It is all very simple if you keep it simple.

People generally do not respond well to the time that procedure and process take. However, I have found that utilizing these principals has helped to minimize anxiety and to make our meetings far less confusing and much more civilized. This new level of civility has clearly helped us to increase our focus upon mission and ministry. People are able to voice their opinions and feel heard, whether things go the way they want or not. This kind of civility in our meetings makes life difficult for the church monster.

ASKING AND ANSWERING TOUGH QUESTIONS

Cannon states, "Debate is the lifeblood of any meeting—the interest, the excitement, the battle—with members matching their ideas and skills." [4]

The problem is not that people have different opinions. Problems develop when members are not given opportunities to hear other perspectives and to vote on the issues. The purpose of the debate that comes after a motion is presented is to help people voice their opinions on any given matter and for the congregation to take the time to think about these opinions and ideas with each other.

It makes sense for congregations to care about the decisions they make. When people have shared fully why they are for or against a particular motion, the congregation should be able to make an informed decision. No one likes it when a motion gets passed that they have spoken against. Nor do they like it when a motion they support is rejected. But everyone feels good about a decision made after a serious level of thoughtful discussion and discernment. When ideas are shared, good questions asked, and serious caution raised in the midst of our discussion, we feel better about making major decisions that demand the commitment of our people.

In addition, when we make ministry-related decisions, we are not just asking what our preferences are. We are asking what the will of God is or where we feel the Holy Spirit is leading us. Although some people do not like some of the decisions made in their churches, if they feel that decisions are made openly and fairly and that people are authentically trying to discern the will of God, they can at least feel good about how the decisions are being made. In Romans 12:2, the apostle Paul writes, "Do not be conformed to this world, but be transformed by the renewing of your minds, so that you may discern what is the will of God—what is good and acceptable and perfect."

REFERENCES TO THE CHURCH BYLAWS

Another discovery we have made at Salem Covenant Church is that people rarely, if ever, feel the need to refer to our constitution and bylaws in our meetings. Because we are taking our congregational polity more seriously than our bylaws require, no one questions by what authority we act. When your members are the ones making the most substantive decisions, they can only mistrust themselves. And if people do not show up for congregational meetings, they are forfeiting their right to voice their opinions and to vote on the issues that are before the congregation.

Matthew 21:23–24 says,

> When Jesus entered the temple, the chief priests and the elders of the people came to him as he was teaching, and said, "By what authority are you doing these things, and who gave you this authority?" Jesus said to them, "I will also ask you one question; if you tell me the answer, then I will also tell you by what authority I do these things."

This is a classic story about the chief priests and elders trying to trick Jesus into saying something that will help them to arrest him and of Jesus turning the table on them with a question for them. They, however, were not concerned about Jesus' credentials. They were concerned about the fact that he was developing more authority than they had outside of "proper channels."

When people in your meetings ask, "What do the bylaws say?" they are typically not concerned with technical precision in following the church constitution. Rather, they are concerned about small groups or individuals making major decisions without consulting the congregation. They are typically frustrated by the way authority is being used and misused in their complicated church systems. How authority is used in our churches does matter. Misusing authority leaves leaders and ideas vulnerable to attack.

CONGREGATIONAL AUTHORITY

This can all be avoided through a radical commitment to making decisions congregationally. When you allow your church members to help make major decisions, they cannot get mad at anyone but themselves. There have been times at Salem Covenant Church when certain individuals have not liked decisions that were made. However, when people who were not at our meetings feel this way and come to me or other church leaders to share their thoughts, feelings, and opinions, we simply ask, "Were you at the meeting?" When they say no, we are then able to say, "That's too bad. It would have been helpful for everyone to have heard your opinions before we made this decision." The discussions typically end there, and we get on with our lives and ministry. We all have one voice and one vote in congregational church polity. However, if you do not attend the meetings, you are unable to use your voice and vote. It is as simple as that.

This kind of governing system keeps any one individual from having too much power in your congregation. One vote, one voice, really works! Some voices may carry more weight than others, but everyone in a system like this begins to realize that we all need to be mature enough to understand things may not always go our way. That goes for pastors and church pillars alike. When we make decisions together on a regular basis, the congregation begins to take its responsibilities and the direction of their church more seriously. The exciting thing about this is that people end up feeling a part of what is taking place. They develop a vested interest in the success of your ministries.

COMMITTEES AND SPECIAL PROJECTS

Committees, like *Robert's Rules*, should also be used as much as necessary but as little as possible. There are times when certain projects need the attention of more than one individual and when the church council will not have the time or energy to address all the issues related to special projects. Committees do serve a purpose. However, when special committees are formed, they should be established with a clear purpose in mind and a specific time frame within which they should complete their work.

The only standing committees in our church are the nominating committee and the stewardship and vision committee. These committees have a clear purpose and clear timetables associated with them. General committees without clear purposes and time frames should be avoided at all cost. It is not prudent, for example, to have a general decorating committee. But if your congregation decides to renovate or redecorate a particular area in your church building, forming a special committee would be essential. Committees work best after congregations have decided on a specific plan or purpose for them. They should be focused on getting something done or on bringing a specific proposal back to the congregation on a specific date. This keeps their work focused and clear. It also sets clear parameters for their meetings and their work. It helps them to meet only as much as necessary and only until their designated job is completed.

DREAMS AND VISIONS

If a church decides not to take a particular step or risk one year, it does not follow that the church will not be able to revisit the idea in the future. Serious decisions need to be made when serious questions are being asked. Thus, all motions presented to the congregation should proceed to a vote. There will always be limits to what we can do congregationally, and no votes make us keenly aware of these limits. Yes votes, in contrast, reveal that sometimes we are able to face challenges cooperatively by making decisions together that we typically would not have made on our own. Asking these difficult questions congregationally keeps the church monster from controlling your church's agenda and sense of direction.

Churches that table decisions more often than they make them are exposing an insecurity with asking difficult questions. Cannon writes, "The Chair should not take a motion to postpone indefinitely, for this motion does no more than negate the main motion in the same way that the amendment to add the word 'not' (at the beginning of the main motion) negates it. Neither motion serves any real purpose. The proper way to defeat a main motion is to vote against it."[5]

Voting no to something someone else believes in can be difficult. This is why serious discussion is so important. If making a decision is difficult, paper ballots can be used to offer some level of confidentiality to those who feel uncomfortable expressing their opinion publicly.

We all need to dream dreams and see visions. To do this, we have to be willing to look beyond that which seems possible in the midst of our current set of circumstances. However, to turn our dreams into realities and our visions into actualities, we have to be willing to ask the question, "Is it time yet?" On certain occasions, the answer may be that it is not. Nevertheless, occasions where the answer is yes are thrilling.

Frank Tillapaugh writes, "There is something valuable about feeling God wants you to do something but you don't yet have the foggiest idea of how to go about it. There is something necessary about making mistakes and experiencing failure."[6]

Discernment is the key to deciding which dreams to follow, and if we never ask tough questions, there will never be any real need for discernment. The best decisions made in congregational meetings are those that even the pastor and church leaders are unsure about. It is when the people of the church pull together and make wise, tough, and courageous decisions that things really begin to move along in our churches.

In *Leadership Is An Art*, Max De Pree writes, "Leaders owe people space, space in the sense of freedom. Freedom in the sense of enabling our gifts to be exercised. We need to give each other the space to grow, to be ourselves, to exercise our diversity. We need to give each other space so that we may both give and receive such beautiful things as ideas, openness, dignity, joy, healing, and inclusion."[7] These things, among others, are what will help us to most effectively challenge the church monster. They will be among the things that we will be able to credit for defeating it and for allowing us to focus on the things that truly matter in our churches.

Voluntary Commitment and Participation

While teaching a new-members class at Salem Covenant Church, a young woman became very concerned about whether or not she would automatically be assigned to a committee once she joined the church. Apparently, she had been involved with a church where the Church Council decided to assign every member to a committee or a board. They did not ask people if they were willing to participate. In her mind, participation on a committee or board was a requirement for membership. I assured her this requirement did not exist at Salem and that she would be asked to do things, not forced to do them.

Motivation for Participation

Congregations are voluntary. You cannot force people to come to your church, and you cannot force people in your church to do anything against their will. Some church leaders discover that guilt can be effective at coercing people to do things. However, over time, these leaders discover that guilt is not an effective long-term motivator. Enthusiasm is far more effective at motivating people to be involved with ministry. If people want to participate in the ministries of your church, they will not only do more, they will also do what they do more effectively.

Frank Tillapaugh writes, "Lasting motivation comes from within. And nothing motivates from within like being involved in a front-line ministry to which God has called us."[1]

Earlier in the same chapter Tillapaugh writes, "If people are doing what God has called them to do, then probably they are doing what they want to do."[2] Working with people to discern what God may be calling them to do is a much more exciting way to motivate people toward ministry than coercion or the use of shame or guilt.

It takes serious, personal discernment to uncover your spiritual gifts and to discover how God is calling you to use them within the body of Christ. One way we can encourage people to participate in this kind of discernment process is to create a sense of mission within our congregations. Developing a sense of mission is essential for motivating people to discern their gifts and to be involved in church ministries. It also helps us to develop and sustain congregational enthusiasm.

William Easum writes about spiritual gifts saying, "Building up the Body of Christ is the goal of spiritual gifts, not meeting the needs of the participants. Their needs are met as they find their God-given place in the Body of Christ. . . . Burnout is minimized because the participants are doing what they enjoy and do well."[3]

Our goal in the church should never be to make everyone happy. However, it is hard to imagine unhappy people doing what they enjoy doing and helping other people while doing it.

Mission Statements and Objectives

Writing a mission statement is one concrete thing you can do to help develop the sense of mission in your church. Mission statements state the obvious as to why you exist as a congregation. They do not have to be flashy, but they do need to be comprehensive and concise. Mission statements allow individuals to comprehend and take ownership of your mission. It is one tool by which you can help make people want to be a part of your ministries. Begin with the words: "Our mission is...." Then finish the sentence.

Kennon Callahan talks about developing "concrete missional objectives." He writes, "Those churches that have been effective in missional outreach have tended to identify very specific human hurts and hopes with which they have shared their principal leadership and financial resources."[4]

He continues saying, "In many local churches, the most effective way to develop mission is to 'grow it up from within.' By inviting members of a congregation to look within themselves at their own longings and strengths to help, it becomes possible to grow the church's mission from within."[5]

Mission and ministry go hand in hand. If you want people to participate in your ministries, you must develop a sense of mission within your congregation. In Matthew 28:18–20, Jesus declared, "All authority in heaven and on earth has been given to me. Go therefore and make disciples of all nations, baptizing them in the name of the Father and of the Son and of the Holy Spirit, and teaching them to obey everything that I have commanded you. And remember, I am with you always, to the end of the age."

This was Jesus' mission statement for the Church. It was his way of calling his disciples and all future followers to continue doing the things he set before us to accomplish.

LEADERS AND LEADERSHIP

When a church is working properly, a nominating committee will seek people with appropriate levels of interest and ability to fill leadership positions. They will not just ask each other who they think might be willing to fill a specific position. Rather, they seek to find the right person for the job. They will look at the temperaments, talents, and spiritual gifts of different individuals. They will not only look at how a person's gifts fit with the specific job requirements but also at how that person seems to fit together with the church council and the needs of the congregation. With a smaller, more centralized church government, the days of persuading people to be on boards with the promise that they won't really have to do anything will be long gone. The people in leadership truly will be leaders.

In *Moving Off the Map,* Thomas Bandy writes, "The thriving church equips people for excellence. They prioritize energy to train individuals to do, with the highest quality of performance and integrity possible, whatever it is Christ calls them to do. They never just accept the best volunteers offer; they assist volunteers to achieve their highest potential service."[6]

At Salem Covenant Church, we have two annual orientation meetings. The first is the previously mentioned Leadership Orientation, for all people in leadership positions. The second is a Sunday School Teacher Orientation at the beginning of September. Both meetings stress the importance of being the best leaders or teachers we can be and help our volunteers feel more confident about what they are doing. In addition, emphasizing the need to approach these positions with some training suggests that there is a right way and a wrong way to do these jobs. It allows us to offer our teachers and leaders boundaries that they would otherwise not have. We have discovered that most people appreciate the boundaries and guidance they receive through these orientation meetings. We serve pizza and salad to ensure that people will come, which also helps to reinforce the importance we place on these meetings and their positions in our church.

RECRUITMENT AND COMMITMENT

With a smaller church government it can still be challenging to find people to fill positions because of how much is required of each individual. However, when you do find someone, they are typically very committed to the task at hand. You may have to put more time and energy into finding these individuals, but once you find them, you'll be glad you did.

Edwin Friedman writes about difficulties with delegation, he writes,

A similar phenomena occurs in work systems where leaders are always trying (usually unsuccessfully) to delegate responsibility. A far more effective form of leadership can be to delegate anxiety: "I just want you all to know that our collections have been so low to this point that we probably won't last to the end of the year. It would be my suggestion, therefore, that we establish a committee to see if we can still get a good price for our building, and merge with our rival across town." Challenge is the basic context of health and survival, of a person, of the family, of a religious organization, or even of an entire species.[7]

When we face challenges like finding people who are willing to be leaders and are willing bear real responsibility, we are called on to embrace the life we are searching for within our congregations. Churches need leaders, and it is essential that nominating committees find people who are willing to lead. Churches do not just need warm bodies to fill vacancies to satisfy church bylaws. They need leaders who will help their church focus upon ministry. Finding people to lead may be a challenge, but filling up our leadership positions with people who do not want to participate, let alone lead, is an even bigger problem. Eventually, the transformation process should lead all of our churches to a place where people are eager to fill these positions and where other people are envious of those who have the privilege of serving in them.

Spiritual Commitment and Community

In *The Different Drum*, M. Scott Peck, best-selling author whose focus is psychological and spiritual issues, writes about community saying, "A group becomes a community in somewhat the same way that a stone becomes a gem—through a process of cutting and polishing."[8]

Writing specifically about commitment in the church, Peck states, "The process of community-building begins with commitment—a commitment of the members not to drop out, a commitment to hang in their through thick and thin, through the pain and chaos of emptiness. The Church has not generally required such commitment. Now the time has come to require it. For without that commitment community is impossible."[9]

Peck accurately identifies the need for commitment within churches, but churches are not in a position to require this kind of commitment. Churches are, however, in a position to inspire it, and the way to do that is to point toward the good things that can come from being a committed member within a community that shares a mutually high-level of commitment to each other and to Christ's mission.

Membership and leadership need to mean something in our churches if our churches hope to have a strong future. Leadership positions within churches ought to be demanding, and people should feel honored by the privilege they have been given to serve Christ and the church through these positions. When we ask people to serve, we are asking them to be a part of something meaningful in a world filled with so many meaningless things.

Bandy writes, "The thriving church perceives membership as a covenant to go deeper in faith, to discern the true origins and purposes behind the changes they are experiencing in life. Church membership moves people into processes of intimacy, mutual support, and personal growth."[10]

Spiritual growth encourages high morale and high levels of participation. When individuals feel that they are growing spiritually and their church is facilitating this spiritual growth, they want to be involved with helping others to have similar experiences. Our ministries need to be relevant to the lives of the individuals in our churches, and they must focus on the heart and hands, not just the head. Bandy writes, "Adult spiritual formation is crucial to the whole because without it neither integrity nor learning can be accomplished."[11]

In Philippians 3:10–11, the apostle Paul writes, "I want to know Christ and the power of his resurrection and the sharing of his sufferings by becoming like him in his death, if somehow I may attain the resurrection from the dead."

When Paul talks about knowing Christ, he is not just talking about head knowledge. He is also talking about a knowledge of the heart. Paul is referring to a faith that affects him internally and which leads him to external action. The people in our churches want their lives to be affected by their involvement. They may resist entering into a process of personal transformation, but, ultimately, they yearn to be transformed.

In Philippians 4:8–9, Paul writes, "Finally beloved, whatever is true, whatever is honorable, whatever is just, whatever is pure, whatever is pleasing, whatever is commendable, if there is any excellence and if there is anything worthy of praise, think about these things. Keep on doing the things that you have learned and received and heard and seen in me, and the God of peace will be with you."

Participation in churches and their ministries is voluntary. There is no way we can force anyone to attend worship or to participate. We must inspire this kind of interest in our ministries through our ministries. Challenging the church monster has a lot to do with inspiring enthusiasm and creating momentum. If we are truly going to defeat this monster, we not only need to change our structure, we also need to change the way we go about doing our ministries. The hope is that new structure will lead into positive new beginnings that will allow us to have a renewed focus on serving people and God.

12

Bottom-Up Leadership

For years, one of the most painfully obvious weaknesses at Salem Covenant Church was in the area of ministry to high school students. There was a relatively active, middle-school youth group and a two-year confirmation-discipleship program that I led on Sunday mornings for seventh- and eighth-graders. Virtually nothing, however, was going on for high school students—not even a high school Sunday-school class. Part of the problem was that people associated confirmation with graduation. During the first few years of teaching confirmation, I sought to destroy this mind association. I taught them that confirmation is a beginning, not an ending.

FROM THE BOTTOM UP

After a few years, I began to see some fruit from this labor when several young people expressed an interest in a high school Sunday-school class the year after their confirmation. Wanting to seize this opportunity, I quickly asked a few capable people if they would be interested in teaching such a class. They said yes, and the ball was rolling. Much to my surprise, however, our Christian-education coordinator became upset with me for not going through her to establish this class. Upon paying a visit to her house to address her concerns, I quickly began to see why she got upset and how differently we were approaching our positions.

Seeing that ministry to high school students was falling through the cracks, I sought to do anything I could to pick up the pieces and make something happen. And though I felt I was boosting the leadership within Christian education, she felt I was overstepping my bounds. We quickly realized we were operating from two very different perspectives. I was approaching things from the bottom-up, whereas she was approaching things top-down. I explained that if I thought for a minute she or anyone else involved with Christian education would have been upset by my actions, I would not have done anything without consulting her and having it approved by the Church Council or the congregation. I simply saw an opportunity to strengthen our ministries and pursued it.

I conveyed to her that I did not expect her or any leader from our church to be able to deal with every issue that arises in their areas of responsibility. I also explained that, as the pastor, I would always be on the lookout for ministry opportunities falling through the cracks. I explained my primary goal was to equip her and lift her up to do as much as possible within her area of ministry. I explained that I would utilize my time and energy to do as much as possible to help our church be the church that God wants us to be. In the end, she clearly understood and felt more comfortable with my approach.

Things would have been better if I had communicated with her before I established a high school Sunday-school class. And I apologized for this. However, I learned something very important from this experience that I would not have learned otherwise. I learned that seeing your realm of authority as a realm of responsibility was the way to shift from a top-down approach to a bottom-up one. Your mindset must be one concerned with action, not control. If someone else is making something happen within your area of responsibility, this should be celebrated, not restricted or held back in any way. Developing authority within your realm of responsibility is a good thing, if used appropriately. However, when authority becomes your focus, you run the risk of neglecting your responsibilities and missing out on good opportunities for mission and ministry.

SERVANT LEADERSHIP

In Matthew 20:25–28, Jesus said, "You know that the rulers of the Gentiles lord it over them, and their great ones are tyrants over them. It will not be so among you; but whoever wishes to be great among you must be your servant, and whoever wishes to be first among you must be your slave; just as the Son of Man came not to be served but to serve, and to give his life a ransom for many."

Servant leadership is a popular concept for church leaders as a result of this passage. Nevertheless, it is important to recognize that Jesus had all the authority in the world while at the same time came "not to be served but to serve." Developing a servant-leadership style does not mean giving up all authority. It simply means we have to use our authority in service and ministry to each other. It takes a strong leader to be a servant leader, just as it takes a strong leader to focus upon responsibility before authority.

Jesus had a bottom-up style of leadership. You could even say the Word becoming flesh was God's way of approaching us from the bottom-up. In Eugene Peterson's vernacular translation of the Bible, he translates John 1:14, "The Word became flesh and blood, and moved into the neighborhood."[1]

In 2 Corinthians 5:21, Paul writes, "For our sake he made him to be sin who knew no sin, so that in him we might become the righteousness of God."

Philippians 2:5–8 says, "Let the same mind be in you that was in Christ Jesus, who, though he was in the form of God, did not regard equality with God as something to be exploited, but emptied himself, taking on the form of a slave, being born in human likeness. And being found in human form, he humbled himself and became obedient to the point of death—even death on a cross."

Our faith is based on bottom-up servant leadership. Philippians 2:3 says, "Do nothing from selfish ambition or conceit, but in humility regard others as better than yourselves." Pastors and lay leaders need to get behind their congregations and encourage them to become the servant communities God desires. We need to utilize bottom-up leadership to encourage a servant atmosphere within our congregations and throughout our ministries. There is no telling what can be accomplished if congregations begin serving God by serving people.

In *The Upside Down Church*, Greg Laurie writes,

Few things in the Bible are more upside down than God's plan to save the world. Think about this for a moment. The all powerful God of the universe chose limited, fallible human beings as His main vehicle to spread the most important message the world has ever known. He could have chosen angels to do the job. He could have parted the clouds and spoken audibly and said something like, "Hello, humanity. I'm God and you're not." In the past

He spoke through a burning bush, appeared in visions, and carved His laws on stone tablets. But in our day He has clearly chosen ordinary men and women to carry His message of salvation to the world.[2]

Sharing Responsibility and Authority

Churches with small, centralized church governments and a radical commitment to making decisions congregationally will find it very difficult to function from a top-down perspective. Leaders in these churches will not want to have the responsibility of looking over the shoulders of those serving with them. Rather, they want to feel the freedom and flexibility that comes from freely sharing responsibility and authority with others.

Our Christian-education coordinator is asked to share a large percentage of his or her authority with the Sunday-school superintendent. They try not to overlap responsibilities. They work independently, but cooperatively, with each other. We have between forty and sixty children in our Sunday school. This is a huge area of responsibility. However, our Christian-education coordinator and our Sunday-school superintendent have discovered that others are willing to share the burdens of leadership with them. They may not be on a board together, and we may not even refer to them as a team, but there is a group of leaders in our Christian-education programs who work cooperatively together.

On occasion, we call a special meeting where we invite everyone interested in Christian education to come and discuss what is taking place and what leadership roles need to be filled. It is less formal, but it works very effectively. Apart from these meetings, most of what needs to be discussed by these leaders happens before or after worship. Or they spend time on the phone together. I also meet occasionally with our Sunday-school superintendent to check in on specific issues and to offer support wherever I can.

To reveal how well this works and how inspiriting this type of leadership can be, I want to share about what took place last summer at our vacation Bible school. We had a little over forty children attend and thirty adults from our church volunteer to help. The director of our vacation Bible school had to turn away volunteers because we had so many interested people. This "problem" confirms for me that people would rather participate in ministry than be on administrative boards. Bottom-up leadership really works. It takes time to change the way people approach leadership, but, once it happens, you will be amazed by the results.

Spiritual Gifts and Abilities

Alvin J. Vander Griend of the Christian Reformed Church writes about why he believes there is a renewed interest of the church in spiritual gifts:

> Many church leaders today are discontented with the structures of the past. They desire to find new and better forms for Christian communal life. Their quest has led them back to the Scriptures for a fresh look at life in the New Testament church. They have concluded that structures based on top-down authority need to be replaced by structures that acknowledge the spiritual giftedness of members.[3]

What we have done at Salem Covenant Church has enabled us to replace a top-down structure with bottom-up one. We have now begun the process of recognizing the spiritual gifts of our members, but we still have a long way to go. Such change cannot happen overnight. Changing your structure is the easy part. Developing a focus upon the gifts of your people is more difficult. All of our churches are filled with untapped potential.

One goal for all church leaders today should be to discover creative ways to invite people to use their spiritual gifts and talents for God's glory. There is so much that can be done in accord with the church's mission, and so much our people have to offer. We simply need to bring these two things together. Vander Griend writes, "Every Christian is full of potential for service in the kingdom. Potential, however, needs to be developed. Unused, it will waste away."[4]

I believe a bottom-up approach to church leadership can help with this. If we use the time and energy people give to the church more effectively, these individuals will start using and developing their spiritual gifts on a more consistent basis.

Smaller church governments with streamlined processes naturally lead into a bottom-up style of church leadership, and a bottom-up style of church leadership naturally leads Christians to utilize their spiritual gifts. When churches are structured properly, people can use their time and talents more effectively. Ministry can become our top priority, and God can be glorified through all we say and do. The church monster will also find it more difficult to hide in a church with a bottom-up style of leadership. Leaders will find that they are sneaking up on the monster, rather than having the monster sneak up on them. Conflict is contained before the monster is able to sink its teeth into our ministries. Creativity and enthusiasm begin to replace the confusion and chaos that used to make the monster feel so much at home in our churches.

13

Innovative and Engaging Worship

Again, one of the first projects we completed together at Salem Covenant Church was the purchase of a new hymnal supplement. The official title of this collection is *The Song Goes On*, but it is affectionately referred to in our church as "the silver book." The silver book was introduced by our denomination as a supplement to our red hymnal before our newer blue hymnals were produced. The silver book is filled with praise songs, new hymns, and cherished old hymns that were dropped from the older green hymnal when the red hymnal was produced. We ordered these silver books three months after I arrived at the church, and when they arrived, we sang all of our congregational hymns from them on the first Sunday to celebrate their arrival. During the next week, I had three or four people approach me to ask if we were ever going to sing out of our red hymnals again. Their response helped me to see that the decisions we make regarding worship can be particularly divisive.

WORSHIP DIVISIONS

Decisions about worship can be this divisive because worship is central to every church's identity. When making these decisions, we need to focus on discernment and the purpose of worship. Some decisions should be brought before the congregation; others should be left up to pastors and worship leaders. Congregations should help to determine the general direction of our worship practices, but they should not be concerned with the specific direction of each worship service. There must be some space allowed for worship planners to surprise and challenge their congregations. Worship should not be stagnant; change and variety help to keep our worship alive and vital. Nevertheless, the changes we introduce do not always help to establish momentum—they can also hinder it. Choosing appropriate ways and times to introduce change is essential. Once again, how we make decisions is often more important than the decisions themselves.

I had an experience at a church I was attending as a young adult that revealed this to me in a poignant way. In the middle of a pastoral transition, the interim pastor came and did not change much in regard to the worship service. However, when the new pastor arrived, he introduced an entirely new order of worship on the first Sunday he was there. My heart sank into my stomach. I left feeling that our church had been judged and deemed unworthy. I could not help but feel upset and angry. It was not that I did not like the changes he made; I could have lived with them. It was how these changes were introduced that upset me.

When I started my ministry at Salem Covenant Church, there were things I would have changed in the worship service on the first Sunday. But as a result of my experience in this other church, I committed myself to not changing much, if anything, about our worship service during my first year. Much to my surprise, I eventually discovered people were eager for some change. This is why we ordered *The Song Goes On* books in my first few months of ministry. And yet, their response, "Are we ever going to sing out of our red hymnals again?" revealed to me how tenuous making changes to the worship service can be. It also made me glad that the decision to order these books was made congregationally.

It is also interesting to note that after getting to know the church and experiencing the worship, I could not believe some of the changes I would have made on that first Sunday if I had been given the opportunity. We have since made several changes to our worship service, but they were not the changes I would have made when I first arrived. Marva Dawn, musician and theologian, writes, "We must plan worship with substance enough to root people in faith, to establish a community of care."[1]

Worship Decisions

Variety, texture, and alternative worship experiences help to keep worship services alive, engaging, and vital. Our worship services must have stability, but they also must have enough depth and texture to connect with a wide range of people and to meet a wide variety of needs. Robert Webber, president of the Institute for Worship Studies, writes in his book *Planning Blended Worship,*

> Good worship creates community, evangelical warmth, hospitality to outsiders, inclusion of cultural diversity, leadership roles for men and women, intergenerational involvement, personal and community formation, healing, reconciliation, and other aspects of pastoral care. Because worship is itself an act of witness, it is the door to church growth, to missions and evangelism, and to issues of social justice. Worship now stands at the center of the Church's life and mission in the world.[2]

At Salem Covenant Church, we have sought to add depth and texture to our worship service in a variety of ways. Some of the ways have been through permanent changes to our worship service; whereas others have been through occasional opportunities for people to experience something extraordinary in worship. One Sunday morning, for example, the focus of our service was on healing, and I asked those in attendance if anyone wanted prayers for healing and invited people to come forward to be anointed with oil. The first time I did this, approximately thirty people came forward. One member came to me after the service to tell me how uncomfortable she was during the service when I introduced this. But she said that when she saw so many people go forward, she could see how some people needed the experience.

I told this story to a pastor friend of mine, and he could not believe I would introduce something like this in worship without first asking for permission. He said, "My deacons would never allow it." When I asked him why not, he said, "They would get anxious about the people who would get upset by something like this." Once again, a few imaginary angry people end up keeping something potentially good from taking place. The limited courage that boards are allowed to have limits the courage pastors and worship leaders are able to embrace.

If I am calling on people to voluntarily participate in an element of worship, I do not ask for permission to do this ahead of time. I know some people will be uncomfortable, and yet I also know they can choose not to participate. When you present opportunities like this, you are challenging people, and when you challenge people, they are bound to feel uncomfortable. But with challenges, spiritual growth is often the outcome.

Making Change

One example of a substantive change I did bring to our congregation for approval is related to the traditional greeting at the beginning of our worship service. This had always been a "good morning" by the pastor and a responsive "good morning" by the congregation. A few years into my ministry, I decided that it would enhance our worship service to add the ancient greeting of "Peace be with you," and the congregational response, "and also with you." Nevertheless, I did not simply introduce this on a Sunday morning. I talked about it with the Church Council and then presented it to the congregation as something with which I would like us to experiment. The congregation approved this on a trial basis during the season of Lent, and then confirmed it at our next congregational meeting. This greeting and response have now become a regular part of our worship service.

Typically, when I suggest adding, subtracting, or altering something in our regular order of worship, I bring these changes to the congregation for approval. Had I not asked for congregational approval before introducing this new greeting, some people may have had an immediate negative reaction simply because it was new and different. They would have asked, "Who made this decision?" The potential for controversy then would have been alive, and the idea left vulnerable.

Asking for approval to change something like this increases the chances of its survival. People enter into it as an experiment. They know it will be different, some even know it will be uncomfortable at first, but they will almost always give it a try. And when someone who was not at the meeting does not like it and asks the question, "Who made this decision?" the answer is, "the congregation." There is then a chance that they, too, will be more willing to experiment with it.

Difficult Change

Change is difficult for almost everyone. Some pastors and leaders mistakenly associate this difficulty with age. They fool themselves into thinking that older members are the only ones uncomfortable with change. Church leaders isolate these members by implying that if the church does not make certain changes, we will never attract young people to our church. Playing the "age card" usually has disastrous results. At Salem Covenant Church, people of all ages enjoy the texture in our worship services. Not everyone likes everything we do, but they participate and their focus is on God, not those making decisions.

Dawn writes, "Because the people who come for worship represent an immense diversity of ages, emotions, concerns, and spiritual maturity, authentic worship requires a variety of musical styles to convey an assortment of moods and convictions."[3]

A few years ago, our church had a work Saturday, where members did odd jobs around and inside the church building. A few women decided that it would be a good idea to rearrange the furniture in the room where I do most of my teaching. This room has a meeting area with a table that seats twelve, and there is a sitting area with a couch, a coffee table, and a few random chairs. These individuals reversed the entire room.

I had grown accustomed to how things were before they started moving things around, and I let them know how I was feeling. We ended up talking about it, and I reluctantly admitted my concerns probably just reflected my discomfort with change. I agreed to give it a chance, but I was also convinced that, at some point in the future, I would end up changing things back to the way things had been. I have since discovered I really like the changes they made. I use the sitting area more often, and the room looks much nicer.

Change is not always easy. When we make decisions to change things about our worship services, we need to be sensitive to the way people will initially react to these changes. Approaching change experimentally gives people the time and space they need to get over the initial shock of the changes, and it gives people the time they need to experiment personally with them. If people know that the church is going to evaluate a change at a later date, they do not feel pressured to pass judgment right away. With time, those initially shocked by the changes may discover that they like the emerging new realities even more than the previous realities to which they had grown so accustomed.

Planning Worship

One of the worst things a church can do to deal with a divisive worship situation is to develop a worship committee with people from the different sides of the issues represented. Such committees reinforce the fact that there are sides and usually end up being compromise committees. They get together and fight over what songs or hymns will be sung and what other elements will be included in, or excluded from, the worship service, and everything in the end gets watered down. These worship services tend to look and feel like Styrofoam— they do not have depth or texture. Pastors, music leaders, and people actively involved in the leadership of worship are those who should be planning worship.

There are ways to include more people in planning and leading worship. One example of this is a type of community prayer where you ask several people from your congregation to prepare a brief prayer based on a specific theme, like adoration and praise, the sick and the suffering, family and friends, our church and the church, our nation and the world, our gratitude and thanksgiving. [4] You establish an order and have people stand and pray their prayers from where they are seated in your sanctuary. We found this type of prayer particularly meaningful on the Sunday after September 11, 2001. One person prayed for the victims and their families, another the rescue workers, another our national and world leaders, and another for world peace.

The goal of worship planning should not be to come up with something everyone can live with. The goal of worship planning should be to come up with something that calls people to engage their hearts and minds in worship. We should not be thinking about what we are doing while we are worshiping. Rather, we should be thinking about and focusing on God. If worship is innovative, it will invite everyone to participate in the worship. It will be spiritually uplifting and nurturing to individuals and the community of faith.

WORSHIPING IN SPIRIT AND IN TRUTH

When Jesus was speaking with the Samaritan woman at the well, she started talking about a worship-related issue. John 4:19–24 says,

> The woman said to him, "Sir, I see that you are a prophet. Our ancestors worshiped on this mountain, but you say that the place where people must worship is in Jerusalem." Jesus said to her, "Woman, believe me, the hour is coming when you will worship the Father neither on this mountain nor in Jerusalem. You worship what you do not know; we worship what we know, for salvation is from the Jews. But the hour is coming, and is now here, when the true worshipers will worship the Father in spirit and truth, for the Father seeks such as these to worship him. God is spirit, and those who worship him must worship in spirit and truth."

The woman at the well was talking about a major division between the Jews and the Samaritans. While believing Jesus was a prophet, she struggled because she could not accept his place of worship. Jesus responded by saying that a day is coming when these things that have divided us for such a long time will no longer divide us. If Jesus could envision worship that could rise above the major divisions that existed between the Jews and the Samaritans, can we not also share in a vision that would allow our churches to rise above the things that tend to divide us?

My hope is that, as congregations become more flexible and experimental, our worship services will become more innovative and engaging. I also hope that if we shape the general direction of our worship services congregationally, people will be able to come to worship focusing on God rather than on how worship was planned. My hope is that people will be more receptive to the creativity and the ministry being extended by their pastors and worship leaders, and that they will understand the need for change and challenge in worship.

Expecting the Unexpected

During my first few years of ministry in Connecticut, the University of Connecticut women's basketball team won their first NCAA national tournament. When they became national champions, the state exploded with enthusiasm. I had never seen anything like it in women's sports. The enthusiasm for the Lady Huskies continues to this day. After their undefeated season and NCAA championship, their coach, Gino Ariema, was asked what made their team so great. Ariema responded by suggesting that when they recruit players, they not only look for talented individuals, but also for young people who are willing to be a small part of something big, rather than a big part of something small.

A PROPER PERSPECTIVE

This approach makes sense not only in the recruitment of basketball players, but also in the development of our understanding of what it means to be a part of the body of Christ. Large and small congregations alike must realize that, if we are going to effectively build up the body of Christ through our local churches, the people in our churches must begin to think about themselves and their congregations as miniscule in comparison with the body of Christ.

Even mega-churches and corporate-size churches must see themselves as a small part of something big to keep a proper perspective on what it means to be a part of the body of Christ.[1] Even though individuals in large churches may be more likely to see themselves individually as a small part of something big, they often underestimate how big the body of Christ is in relationship to their congregations. It is important to keep a proper perspective with regard to what it means to be a part of the body of Christ.

Robert Slocum distinguishes between the "Church Gathered" and the "Church Scattered." Slocum identifies the Church Gathered as, "the people of God gathered as a local congregation," and the Church Scattered as, "the people of God scattered into the world." We need to know that, no matter what size our congregations are, we are also members of the Church Scattered, not merely a "Church Gathered."[2]

Many congregations are plagued by individuals who believe they are a big part of a small thing. These individuals tend to overestimate what they are capable of doing and underestimate the capabilities of others. They leave little room for the influence of others and the influence of God. Individuals in your church who see themselves as a big part of something small are heading down a dark and dangerous path. This type of thinking may not only affect them as individuals, but also your congregation as a whole.

On the other hand, when people develop approaches where they see themselves as a small part of something big, they not only leave more room for God to work in their local churches but also for God to work dramatically in their own lives. Through our local churches, we enter into the business of changing lives and transforming our society and world. When individuals recognize the magnitude of the church's mission, God begins to work powerfully through the hearts and the lives of his people. We can change the world through the local church, but we need to realize that we do this one person at a time and by faithfully serving him through the worship and ministry to which we are called in the local church.

In Galatians 6:2–5, Paul writes, "Bear one another's burdens, and in this way you will fulfill the law of Christ. For if those who are nothing think they are something, they deceive themselves. All must test their own work, rather than their neighbor's work; then that work, rather than their neighbor's work, will become a cause for pride. For all must carry their own loads."

STRUCTURE AND SUBSTANCE

Herb Miller, executive director of the National Evangelism Association of the Christian Church, talks about five activities in which all Christians should be engaged: "worship, learning, fellowship, witness, and service."[3] I would add prayer as a sixth element to this list. Prayer, study, worship, fellowship, evangelism, and ministry—these are the things on which our churches should be focused. If our time and energy is being directed elsewhere, we are paying attention to the wrong things.

This book focuses on structure primarily to ensure that bad structure does not interfere with the substance of church life. The structure of our churches is secondary to the substance that underlies each church's existence. Congregations need to collectively come to a clearer understanding of the substantive reasons for their existence. We exist for discipleship, worship, and ministry. We do not exist to take care of buildings, budgets, and bureaucracies.

The people of Salem Covenant Church do not go around talking about church structure all the time. Church leaders are clearly aware of our church structure and how things work. All new members are informed about how we make decisions and why we are structured in this way. However, most of the people in our church spend very little time thinking about system issues. This is exactly how it ought to be. Individuals in the church parking lot should be discussing personal, social, and spiritual issues, not church government and administration.

The institutional approach to "being the church" is dying a slow and painful death. The people-of-God approach has been alive ever since the origins of the Christian Church, and this approach will once again help rekindle the fire that will allow the Christian faith to burn in our hearts for generations to come. Institutional churches can reorient themselves and become focused on being the people of God. Churches can become more focused on ministry and less focused on meetings, more focused on worship and less focused on church government.

A RADICAL CALLING

Several years ago, I had an opportunity to hear best-selling author Keith Miller speak about his understanding of the church. Many of the things he said helped me to refocus my attention on ministry and to expand my enthusiasm for the future of the church. Miller suggested that churches should not just be seen as places to go and get healed but rather as "creative centers for life." He suggested that churches should not be like "drum and bugle corps" but rather like "full blown orchestras." The implications of his comments were that churches ought to be places that celebrate life, creativity, and diversity; and that our ministries ought to be unique, alive, and inviting.[4] We need to be clear about our purpose but also flexible in how we act on these purposes. We need to offer love, acceptance, and the opportunity for all people to encounter the presence and power of God through the love that comes from Christ Jesus and from being a part of the body of Christ.

In *Evangelism that Works,* George Barna writes, "Sociologists have described America as the loneliest nation on the face of the earth. Our research suggests they may be right. Although we live in close proximity to tens of thousands of people and probably come in contact with hundreds of people every week, most of us have few real friends, few true confidants."[5]

Most churches in the United States describe themselves as friendly, which is nice. But is it enough? A few years ago, our church participated in a leadership retreat where the presenter stated that there was a big difference between being friendly and making friends.[6] This challenging statement begged the questions, "Are we creating environments in our churches where people can form real and lasting friendships? Are we getting to know each other in our churches, or are we simply being nice to each other?" True fellowship will only develop in our churches when real and lasting relationships are formed. Being nice is not enough.

Scott Peck writes, "As I travel through the country, I find many of the clergy in a state of despair. Most are intensely aware of a lack of community in their congregations. They suffer it not only in their role as leaders but also as individual humans. They do not feel in community with their own congregations."[7]

I find this to be a sad commentary on the state of the church today and on the place where many Christian ministers find themselves. My optimistic nature leads me to believe things can be different, and many of my experiences at Salem Covenant Church have validated my view and left me feeling hopeful.

Salem Covenant Church is not a perfect church, but we have allowed ourselves to begin thinking about what it means to be the body of Christ and what it means to be a part of a Christian community. We are not trying to be all things to all people, but we are trying to make all people feel welcome, and we are trying to stay open to the potential for God's involvement in their lives, in our lives, and in the life of our congregation.

With regard to churches, 1 Peter 2:9 states, "You are a chosen race, a royal priesthood, a holy nation, God's own people, in order that you may proclaim the mighty acts of him who called you out of darkness into his marvelous light."

There will always be a gap between the way our churches are and the way they ought to be. However, this should not keep us from striving forward. We are all a small part of something much bigger. We are a part of God's work in our world. We are a people with a magnificent purpose. We have been called to proclaim the mighty acts of God. This is a radical calling which demands a radical commitment on our part.

WORKING TOGETHER

I passionately believe that bad structure is keeping our churches from being the churches God wants them to be in this day and age. God wants us to be passionate about God's purposes and free from the anxiety that has kept this from taking place. Infighting and nonsensical conflicts must end. New ways must be implemented to deal with our conflicts and to make decisions more effectively and efficiently. And we must begin to see our call to the mission, worship, and unity of the church as central for our lives and the lives of our congregations.

We need to be hope-filled. To be effective in ministry and leadership we have to learn how to expect the unexpected. We never know when opportunities will present themselves or when new beginnings in our churches will take place. I have encountered several people through my ministry at Salem Covenant Church who were in life-threatening situations. In a few of these situations, I was even beginning to think about their funerals before I should have, and then in accordance with the way God often seems to work, God surprised me. God surprised us with life. And in the same way God may surprise you and your churches with life. God likes to surprise us, and if you are feeling discouraged, my hope is that God will surprise you.

In Super Bowl XXXVI, the New England Patriots unexpectedly beat the St. Louis Rams, with the youngest quarterback to ever lead a team to a Super-Bowl victory. However, the defining moment in this game took place before the game even began. The New England Patriots chose to be introduced as a team rather than to have each player introduced individually. As a team, they stormed onto the field together. They may not have matched up one by one with the Rams, but they came out played as a team and won the game.

We in the church must decide to work together as a team. Developing a downsized and centralized church government, together with a radical commitment to making decisions congregationally, will help your churches to function as a team and to have a proper focus upon mission and ministry. You will have fewer meetings and more ministry, less conflict and more community. You will more naturally see yourselves as a small part of something big; rather than as a big part of something small. And my hope is that in time all your people will discover they like this new emerging reality, even more than the old reality to which they had grown so accustomed. My hope is that this new reality will help you to defeat the church monster and that your new focus will be on worship, ministry, and community.

Benediction

Now to him who by the power at work within us is able to accomplish abundantly far more than all we can ask or imagine, to him be glory in the church and in Christ Jesus to all generations, forever and ever. Amen!
                                    —Ephesians 3:20–21

Notes

Foreword

1. For an outline of this strategy and its rationale, see Ichak Adizes, *Corporate Lifecycles: How and Why Corporations Grow and Die and What to Do about It,* (Englewood Cliffs: Prentice Hall, 1988), esp. 87–88, 337 ff.

2. For an elaboration of Weber's foundational insights about movements and institutions, see "The Nature of Charismatic Domination," *Max Weber: Selections in Translation,* ed. W. G. Runciman, trans. Eric Matthews (Cambridge: Cambridge University Press, 1978), 226–50.

3. A sampling of such research publications includes R. Stephen Warner, *New Wine in Old Wineskins: Evangelicals and Liberals in a Small-Town Church,* (Berkeley: University of California Press, 1988); James P. Wind and James W. Lewis, eds., *American Congregations: Portraits of Twelve Religious Communities,* vol. 1, and *American Congregations: New Perspectives in the Study of Congregations,* vol. 2 (Chicago: The University of Chicago Press, 1994); and, as an example of applied research, C. Kirk Hadaway, *What Can We Do about Church Dropouts?* (Nashville, Tenn.: Abingdon, 1990). Studies that relate congregations to broader trends in American religion include Wade Clark Roof and William McKinney, *American Mainline Religion: Its Changing Shape and Future* (New Brunswick: Rutgers University Press, 1987) and David A. Roozen and C. Kirk Hadaway, eds. *Church and Denominational Growth: What Does (and Does Not) Cause Growth or Decline* (Nashville, Tenn.: Abingdon, 1993).

4. For help on walking your church through a process to clarify and use fresh vision, see George B. Thompson Jr., *Futuring Your Church: Finding Your Vision and Making It Work* (Cleveland: United Church Press, 1999).

Introduction

1. George Barna, *Evangelism That Works: How to Reach Changing Generations with the Unchanging Gospel* (Ventura, Calif.: Regal Books, 1995), 51.

2. Ibid., 50.

3. Ibid.

Chap. 1: The Anxiety Frenzy

1. William Easum, *Dancing with Dinosaurs: Ministry in a Hostile and Hurting World* (Nashville, Tenn.: Abingdon, 1993), 29.

2. Ibid., 80.

3. Marshall Shelley, *Well-Intentioned Dragons: Ministering to Problem People in the Church* (Waco, Texas: Word Books, 1985), 83.

Chap. 2: The Overly Organized Church

1. Marshall Shelley, *Well-Intentioned Dragons,* 86–87.

2. Ibid., 85.

3. Ibid., 86.

4. Kennon L. Callahan, *Twelve Keys to an Effective Church* (San Francisco: Harper & Row, 1983), 62.
5. Ibid., 59.
6. Thomas G. Bandy, *Moving Off the Map: A Field Guide to Changing the Congregation* (Nashville, Tenn.: Abingdon, 1998), 116.

CHAP. 3: DOWNSIZING AND CENTRALIZING
1. Carl S. Dudley and David A. Roozen, "Faith Communities Today," coordinated by the Hartford Institute for Religion Research, Hartford Seminary, 2000. Can be found on and downloaded from the Web site <http://fact.hartsem.edu>. This exhaustive study reveals that half of all congregations in the Untied States have fewer than one hundred regularly participating adults.
2. Rick Warren, *The Purpose-Driven Church: Growth without Compromising Your Message and Mission* (Grand Rapids, Mich.: Zondervan, 1995), 343.
3. Robert E. Slocum, *Maximize Your Ministry: How You as a Lay Person Can Impact Your World for Jesus Christ* (Colorado Springs, Colo.: NavPress, 1990), 8.
4. Ibid., 55.
5. Greg Laurie with David Kopp, *The Upside-Down Church* (Wheaton, Ill.: Tyndale House, 1999), 219.
6. Frank R. Tillapaugh, *Unleashing the Church: Getting People Out of the Fortress and Into Ministry* (Ventura, Calif.: Regal Books, 1982, 1985), 122–23.

CHAP. 4: A RADICAL COMMITMENT
1. Callahan, *Twelve Keys to an Effective Church*, 55.
2. Ibid., 62.

CHAP. 5: PERSUADING YOUR PEOPLE
1. Callahan, *Twelve Keys to an Effective Church*, 59.
2. G. Lloyd Rediger, *Clergy Killers: Guidance for Pastors and Congregations under Attack* (Louisville, Ky.: Westminster John Knox Press, 1997), 2.
3. Ibid.
4. Loren B. Mead, *The Once and Future Church: Reinventing the Congregation for a New Mission Frontier* (Washington, D.C.: Alban Institute, 1991), 40.
5. Ibid., 41.
6. Ibid., 40–41.
7. Ibid., 58.

CHAP. 6: REALISTIC EXPECTATIONS
1. Loren B. Mead, *Transforming Congregations for the Future* (Bethesda, Md.: Alban Institute, 1994), 100.
2. Tillapaugh, *Unleashing the Church*, 129.
3. Edwin H. Friedman, *Generation to Generation: Family Process in Church and Synagogue* (New York: Guilford Press, 1985), 35–36.
4. Ibid., 39.
5. Easum, *Dancing with Dinosaurs*, 5.

CHAP. 7: DRAMATIC CHANGE

1. Easum, *Dancing with Dinosaurs*, 45.
2. Mead, *Transforming Congregations for the Future*, x.
3. Bandy, *Moving Off the Map*, 116.
4. Easum, *Dancing with Dinosaurs*, 54.

CHAP. 8: COURAGEOUS CONGREGATIONS

1. Bandy, *Moving Off the Map*, 31.
2. Ibid., 115.
3. Callahan, *Twelve Keys to an Effective Church*, xvi.
4. Ibid., xvii.
5. Ibid., xviii.

CHAP. 9: UNSTOPPABLE MOMENTUM

1. Max De Pree, *Leadership Is an Art* (New York: Doubleday, 1989), 17.
2. George Parsons, "Changing Congregational Systems," seminar presented at the Midwinter Conference of the Evangelical Covenant Church in Chicago, Ill., Feb. 2–3, 1994.
3. Easum, *Dancing with Dinosaurs*, 111.
4. Tillapaugh, *Unleashing the Church*, 69.
5. Warren, *The Purpose-Driven Church*, 28.
6. Bandy, *Moving Off the Map*, 278.
7. Tillapaugh, *Unleashing the Church*, 73.
8. Bandy, *Moving Off the Map*, 268.

CHAP. 10: MEANINGFUL MEETINGS

1. Hugh Cannon, *Cannon's Concise Guide to Rules of Order* (Boston: Houghton Mifflin, 1995), xix.
2. Ibid., 57.
3. Ibid., 96.
4. Ibid., 107.
5. Ibid., 105.
6. Tillapaugh, *Unleashing the Church*, 139.
7. De Pree, *Leadership Is an Art*, 16–17.

CHAP. 11: VOLUNTARY COMMITMENT AND PARTICIPATION

1. Tillapaugh, *Unleashing the Church*, 131.
2. Ibid., 130.
3. Easum, *Dancing with Dinosaurs*, 74.
4. Callahan, *Twelve Keys to an Effective Church*, 2.
5. Ibid., 4–5.
6. Bandy, *Moving Off the Map*, 74.
7. Friedman, *Generation to Generation*, 49–50.
8. M. Scott Peck, *The Different Drum: Community Making and Peace* (New York: Simon and Schuster, 1987), 60.
9. Ibid., 300.
10. Bandy, *Moving Off the Map*, 67.
11. Ibid., 277.

CHAP. 12: BOTTOM-UP LEADERSHIP

1. Eugene H. Peterson, *The Message: New Testament with Psalms and Proverbs* (Colorado Springs, Colo.: NavPress, 1993), 219.
2. Laurie, *Upside-Down Church*, 57.
3. Alvin J. Vander Griend, *Discover Your Gifts and Learn How to Use Them*, Student Manual (Grand Rapids, Mich.: CRC Publications, 1996), 15. This is a useful resource for teaching people about and helping them to discover their gifts.
4. Ibid., 7.

CHAP. 13: INNOVATIVE AND ENGAGING WORSHIP

1. Marva J. Dawn, *Reaching Out without Dumbing Down: A Theology of Worship for the Turn-of-the-Century Culture* (Grand Rapids, Mich.: Wm. B. Eerdmans, 1995), 292.
2. Robert E. Webber, *Planning Blended Worship: The Creative Mixture of Old and New* (Nashville, Tenn.: Abingdon, 1998), 29.
3. Dawn, *Reaching Out without Dumbing Down*, 179–80.
4. Webber, *Planning Blended Worship*, 119.

CHAP. 14: EXPECTING THE UNEXPECTED

1. George Parsons and Speed B. Leas, *Understanding Your Congregation as a System: The Manual* (Bethesda, Md.: Alban Institute, 1993), 129. This book offers descriptions and definitions for several different size churches. They identify "Corporate-Size Congregations" as those with more than 350 in attendance on a Sunday.
2. Slocum, *Maximize Your Ministry*, 7.
3. Herb Miller, *How to Build a Magnetic Church* (Nashville, Tenn.: Abingdon, 1987), 56.
4. Keith Miller at Trinity Episcopal Church in Newtown, Connecticut. *What Do You Want to do with the Rest of Your Life,* March 19–20, 1995.
5. Barna, *Evangelism That Works*, 149.
6. Larry Leonard, *Lay Renewal Ministries Leadership Seminar*, March 21–22, 1997.
7. Peck, *The Different Drum*, 301.

Bibliography

Bandy, Thomas G. *Moving Off the Map: A Field Guide to Changing the Congregation.* Nashville, Tenn.: Abingdon Press, 1998.

Barna, George. *Evangelism That Works: How to Reach Changing Generations with the Unchanging Gospel.* Ventura, Calif.: Regal Books, 1995.

Callahan, Kennon L. "Calling the Plays Players Can Run." *Leadership* 12, no 2 (spring 1991): 16–25.

————. *Twelve Keys to an Effective Church.* San Francisco: Harper & Row, 1983.

Cannon, Hugh. *Cannon's Concise Guide to Rules of Order.* Boston: Houghton Mifflin, 1995.

Dawn, Marva J. *Reaching Out without Dumbing Down: A Theology of Worship for the Turn-of-the-Century Culture.* Grand Rapids, Mich.: William B. Eerdmans, 1995.

De Pree, Max. *Leadership Is an Art.* New York: Doubleday, 1989.

Easum, William. *Dancing with Dinosaurs: Ministry in a Hostile and Hurting World.* Nashville, Tenn.: Abingdon, 1993.

Friedman, Edwin H. *Generation to Generation: Family Process in Church and Synagogue.* New York: Guilford Press, 1985.

Laurie, Greg, with David Kopp. *The Upside-Down Church.* Wheaton, Ill.: Tyndale House, 1999.

Mead, Loren B. *The Once and Future Church: Reinventing the Congregation for a New Mission Frontier.* Washington, D.C.: Alban Institute, 1991.

————. *Transforming Congregations for the Future.* Bethesda, Md.: Alban Institute, 1994.

Miller, Herb. *How to Build a Magnetic Church.* Nashville, Tenn.: Abingdon, 1987.

Parsons, George, and Speed B. Leas. *Understanding Your Congregation as a System: The Manual.* Bethesda, Md.: Alban Institute, 1993.

Peck, M. Scott. *The Different Drum: Community Making and Peace*. New York: Simon and Schuster, 1987.

Peterson, Eugene H. *The Message: New Testament with Psalms and Proverbs*. Colorado Springs, Colo.: NavPress, 1993.

Rediger, G. Lloyd. *Clergy Killers: Guidance for Pastors and Congregations Under Attack*. Louisville, Ky.: Westminster John Knox Press, 1997.

Shelley, Marshall. *Well-Intentioned Dragons: Ministering to Problem People in the Church*. Waco, Texas: Word Books, 1985.

Slocum, Robert E. *Maximize Your Ministry: How You as a Lay Person Can Impact Your World for Jesus Christ*. Colorado Springs, Colo.: Navpress, 1993.

Tillapaugh, Frank R. *Unleashing the Church: Getting People Out of the Fortress and Into Ministry*. Ventura, Calif.: Regal Books, 1985.

Vander Griend, Alvin J. *Discover Your Gifts and Learn How to Use Them*, Student Manual. Grand Rapids, Mich.: CRC Publications, 1996.

Warren, Rick. *The Purpose-Driven Church: Growth without Compromising Your Message and Mission*. Grand Rapids, Mich.: Zondervan, 1995.

Other books from
The Pilgrim Press

The Generation-Driven Church
Evangelizing Boomers, Busters, and Millennials
WILLIAM BENKE AND LE ETTA BENKE

The Benkes seek to revitalize the ministries of small and midsize churches by helping them to adjust to the changing culture. This book offers strategic approaches that will reorient ministries to attract younger generations and take churches with an "inward focus" (churches devoid of conversion growth because of the absence of meaningful outreach to unchurched adults who comprise the postmodernist cultures) to an "outreach focus."

ISBN 0-8298-1509-0/paper/128 pages/$13.00

Behold I Do a New Thing
Transforming Communities of Faith
C. KIRK HADAWAY

Recent talk and thinking about congregations concentrate on declining church attendance. Author Kirk Hadaway thinks an important part of the conversation is missing—how can churches, in spite of the decline, remain engaged in the mission of transforming lives? Looking at churches in new ways and holding new expectations will allow church leadership to guide congregations in the journey where transformation and renewal is constant and embraced.

ISBN 0-8298-1430-2/paper/160 pages/$15.00

How to Get Along with Your Church
Creating Cultural Capital for Ministry
GEORGE B. THOMPSON JR.

This resource incorporates Thompson's research and observations on pastoring a church. He finds that the pastors who are most successful in engaging their parishioners are the ones who develop "cultural capital" within their congregations, meaning that they invest themselves deeply into how their church does its work and ministries.

ISBN 0-8298-1437-X/paper/176 pages/$17.00

Futuring Your Church
Finding Your Vision and Making It Work
GEORGE B. THOMPSON JR.

This book encourages church leaders to explore their congregation's heritage, its current context, and its theological bearings. Thompson provides in-sights that enable church members to discern what God is currently calling the church to do in this time and place. It is a practical, helpful tool for futuring ministry.

ISBN 0-8298-1331-4/paper/128 pages/$14.95

The Big Small Church Book
DAVID R. RAY

Over sixty percent of churches have fewer than seventy-five people in attendance each Sunday. *The Big Small Church Book* contains information on everything from practical business matters to spiritual development for small-membership churches. Clergy and lay leaders of big churches can learn much here as well.

ISBN 0-8298-0936-8/paper/256 pages/$15.95

Legal Guide for Day-to-Day Church Matters
A Handbook for Pastors and Church Leaders
CYNTHIA S. MAZUR AND RONALD K. BULLIS

This book belongs on every pastor's desk, because the church is not exempt from the growing number of lawsuits filed each year. The authors are clergy as well as attorneys.

ISBN 0-8298-0990-2/paper/148 pages/$6.95

To order these or any other books from The Pilgrim Press, call or write to:

The Pilgrim Press
700 Prospect Avenue East
Cleveland, Ohio 44115-1100

Phone orders: 800.537.3394 • Fax orders: 216.736.2206
Please include shipping charges of $4.00 for the first book and 75¢ for each additional book. Or, order from our Web sites at <www.pilgrimpress.com> and <www.ucpress.com>.

Prices subject to change without notice.